Universals and Property Instances

John Bacon

Universals and Property Instances

The Alphabet of Being

Aristotelian Society Series

Volume 15

BLACKWELL
Oxford UK & Cambridge USA

Copyright © John Bacon 1995

The right of John Bacon to be identified as author of this work has been asserted in accordance with the Copyright, Designs and Patents Act 1988.

First published 1995

Blackwell Publishers, the publishing imprint of
Basil Blackwell Inc.
238 Main Street
Cambridge, Massachusetts 02142
USA

Basil Blackwell Ltd
108 Cowley Road
Oxford OX4 1JF
UK

Library of Congress Cataloging in Publication Data
Bacon, John, 1940–
    Universals and property instances: the alphabet of being/John Bacon.
        p.   cm. – (Aristotelian Society series; v. 15)
    Includes bibliographical references and index.
    ISBN 0-631-19629-3 (alk. paper)
    1. Whole and parts (Philosophy)   2. Individuation (Philosophy)
    3. Metaphysics.   I. Title.   II. Series.
    BD396.B32   1995
    111 – dc20
                                                                94-28779
                                                                CIP

British Library Cataloguing in Publication Data
A CIP catalogue record for this book is available from the British Library.

Typeset in 11 on 13 pt Plantin by Best-set Typesetter Ltd., Hong Kong
Printed in Great Britain by Hartnolls Ltd, Bodmin, Cornwall
This book is printed on acid-free paper

Contents

Preface

The gestation of this essay coincides with my career in philosophy. As a student of Wilfrid Sellars at Yale (1962–3), I was fascinated by his essay "Abstract entities" (1963). Unlike Sellars, I became convinced that universals are state-of-affairs types – types in the neo-Peircean sense with states of affairs as their tokens. Later, translating Paul Lorenzen's (1965) suggested to me the construction of types as equivalence classes abstracted on the basis of an invariance (equivalence) relation. With that I had the essential core of trope theory: universals as bundles of tropes ("states of affairs", as I thought of them) generated by an equivalence relation.

However, my attempts to pull this together into a theory of universals kept hitting snags, as reported in my dissertation (1966, ch. 4), and later in a research monograph (1971). The latter was based on an abortive book, *The Universal Abstracted*, begun in Jerusalem in 1969 partly under the supervision of Yehoshua Bar-Hillel. Later I mined the 1971 monograph for the articles (1973) and (1974). The snags resulted from my continued attempts to construe the token-type relation (under Sellars' influence) as basically that of Leo to the lion. This made the whole enterprise dependent upon a satisfactory theory of generic terms, to which I have come only much later (unpublished).

That generic terms could be bypassed became clear to me when my Sydney colleagues finally acquainted me with the work of G. F. Stout (who, as it happens, spent his final years in Sydney) and D. C. Williams. Then everything began to fall into place. I greatly regret not having had Williams (1953) to read alongside Sellars

(1963) as the seed was being planted. (Coincidentally, both papers have since been reprinted in the same book series by Charles C Thomas.)

The wide arc from germination to fruition of this project has taken me from Jerusalem to Jerusalem. The hospitality of the Philosophy Department there has twice nurtured my thinking about universals and states of affairs. And when the muse fell silent, a look out my study window or a short walk from my door brought back the words of David: "I will lift up mine eyes unto the hills, from whence cometh my help." So while the finishing touches were applied in Sydney, the first full draft of this book, like the first attempt twenty years earlier, took shape in the embattled City of Peace.

Although not, I hope, extravagant, this work is animated by a vaguely platonistic, anti-reductionist cast of mind. Call me old-fashioned, but I've never understood what could motivate serious thinkers to undertake the hard work of philosophy just in order to discover how little there is, and how boring *that* is. Let us leave them to their desert landscapes and emulate their rigor.

Along the way, certain friends and colleagues have been particularly helpful with the kind of discussion and criticism that moves one to take one's work seriously and to press on. First there has been Eddy Zemach, right from our first class with Sellars down to the present moment. I am likewise grateful to Milton Fisk, Richmond H. Thomason, Marcelo Dascal, Philip G. Hugly, Abigail L. Rosenthal, Keith Campbell, and David Armstrong. Special thanks are due to Graham Priest, who read the penultimate draft for the Aristotelian Society and made many valuable suggestions. I want to thank Rachel Amir, Secretary of the Philosophy Department at the Hebrew University, for her cheerful support, particularly in contending with the formidable photocopying bureaucracy there.

This work grew up with my children, David and Sara, to whom it is dedicated.

John Bacon
Sydney

Special Symbols

A Alphabetic Symbols

Symbol	§ 1st used	Explanation
		A
α	4B2	the actual world
$\dot{a}$	2C2	trope representing individual a
$\mathscr{A}$	4D6	alternative set of
$\forall$	3D6	for all
ab	5B10	individual $\{A, B\}$
AD	5B10	property $\{A, D\}$
a^i	2B5	a's i-bundle
Av	6A2	11th month in Jewish lunar calendar
		B
B	7B1	believes
B	1A3	basic particular situations (Cresswell)
		C
c	8A10	sufficient cause
–c	8A6	veridically causes
		D
D	4D2	denotes
$\mathscr{D}$	7B1	doxastic alternative set of

D^n	4B2	sets of n-concurrence bundles of tropes
Δ	7B1	doxastic accessibility

E

E_w	1E8	exists in world w
e	2B8	exemplifies, instantiates
$\in$	1D1	member of (a set)
$\exists$	2C3	there are
$\mathscr{E}(a)$	6B2	essence (essential tropes) of a
$\mathscr{E}_\tau(a)$	6B2	essential temporal tropes of a

F

F	4A2	false (truth-value)

H

H	1D2	like (tropes)
h	7A8	var. over likeness relations

I

I	1E2	concurrent (tropes)
I	7A9	self- (Quinean predcate functor)
I^i	2B3	concurrent in ith place
ι	4B2	unit-class of (singleton forming functor)
ι	2B8	the (take singleton to sole member)

J

$\mathscr{J}$	4B5	set of concurrence relations

K

K	4B5	set of world cores
k	4A2	var. over possible-world cores

L

L	8A7	laws of nature
Λ	1C2	empty set
$\lambda x(\ldots x \ldots)$	3A8	the function from x to $(\ldots x \ldots)$

M

M	4D4	von Wright's modal logic without reduction principles

O

O	9A4	ought
O	3D5	occurs (Lewis)
$\bigcirc$	1E7	overlapping (sets)

P

$\dot{P}$	2C1	trope representing property P
$\mathscr{P}$	5C4	particularist structure
$\bar{P}$	3A3	non-P
P_w	3A2	property P localized to world w
$p^=$	7A9	$\{w: p(w, w)\}$
¶	6B3, 3D8	part of; part no.
¶ ¶	3B5	proper part of

Q

Q	9A2	quality (of a trope)
Q3	4B4	like **Q5** but with quant. confined to existents
Q4	4B4	modal logic with variables over world-lines
Q5	4B4	modal logic with rigid variables

R

R^2	2A5	dyadic-relation variable
R^n	2B8	n-adic-relation variable
$\vec{R}$	4B2	that which bears R to
$\langle R^n, a_1, \ldots, a_n \rangle$	3D8, 5C5	constituent sequence ("state of affairs")
$R``X$	4A2	set of things that R an X

S

\$	4B7	straight (world-line as rigidly designated)
Σ	9A4	worse (world) than (deontic accessibility)
$\overleftarrow{\Sigma}`$	9A4	deontic alternative set of

§	2B8	-ing (nominalizer)
§	1A7	section (para.) no.
$\mathscr{SA}$	5C5	substance–attribute structure
$\mathscr{ST}$	5C7	substance–trope structure
S5★	4B3	Kripke's first quantified modal logic

T

T	3D4	set of all tropes (or trope singletons)
T	4A2	true (truth-value)
T	4D4	Feys's equivalent of **M**
$\mathscr{T}$	5C6	trope structure
$\mathfrak{T}$	6A9	time of (trope, state of affairs, or individual)
t	3D5	trope variable
†	7A9	true at $\langle w, w \rangle$ (Lewis)
$[t]$	3D5, 7A10	set of all t-worlds; simple state of affairs
T^2	5A8	set of 2nd-level tropes (hypertropes)
T_n	4B2	set of all n-adic tropes

U

U	4B5	universe of world-lines
$\mathscr{U}$	5C4	universalist structure
∪	2A5	union (of sets or relations)
⋃	4B2	generalized union
⋃"	3A6	set of unions of a member of

V

∨	2A5	or (sentence disjunction)
∨	3A4	property disjunction

W

W	3D5	set of all possible worlds
w	1E7	possible-world variable

X

×	2A5	Cartesian product

| X | 7B7 | dyadic connective placeholder |
| Ξ^n | 2B6 | universal n-adic relation |

B   Arbitrary Symbols

{ }	1C2, 1D3	set of items listed
$\subseteq$	1D1	subset of (a set)
$\subset$	1D1	proper subset of
$\cap$	1E7	intersection (of sets or relations)
$=_{df}$	1E7	is defined as
&	2A5	and
$\langle\ ,\ \rangle$	2A5	ordered pair
$\langle x_1, x_2, \ldots, x_n \rangle$	2B5	n-tuple; finite sequence $x_1, x_2, \ldots, x_n$
$\hat{x}_1 \ldots \hat{x}_n\,(—)$	2B6	abstract of relation in intension
$\{x_1, \ldots, x_n{:}—\}$	2B6	abstract of relation in extension
$\rightarrow$	2B6	if . . . then
↿	2C3	left confinement (of a relation)
$\mid$	2C3	relative product
$X - Y$	3A3	set X minus set Y
2^X	3A5	power set of X
$X \cdot Y$	3A6	set of unions of an X with a Y
$\sim$	3D5	not
$\bigcap$	3D5	generalized intersection
$[w]$	3D5	set of worlds overlapping w (a state of affairs)
④	4D5	**S4** necessity
⟐	4D5	**S4** possibility
$\square$	4D7	necessarily
$\lozenge$	4D7	possibly
$<$	6A5	wholly precedes
$<>$	6A6	wholly before or after
$<>_\ast$	6A6	cotemporal
$\sqcap$	6A6	temporally overlapping
$+$	4B3	mereological sum
$\mid\ \mid_w$	7B1	value in w of

⊩	7B5, 5A6	(strictly) implies (state-of-affairs inclusion)
⊫	7B5	entails (propositional inclusion)
→	7B6	material conditional
−‖−	7B8	logical equivalence
∴	8A6	therefore
□→	8A7	subjunctive conditional (Lewis)
∨	8A10	generalized conjunction

1

Tropes, Universals, and Individuals

1A Tropes and their Uses

1A1 Particularized relations, or tropes

We know some things about our world. I know that I'm now writing at my desk, that I had an egg for breakfast, that London is in England. My knowing these things doesn't consist merely in my thinking that they are so and projecting that thought outward. The world is for the most part not of my making. Rather, the way the world is makes some of my thoughts knowledge.

When we know something about the world, what sort of thing is it that we know? What sort of thing is London's being in England? It isn't just an individual object or a property or a relation. It's a *relating of* two things, a particularized relation. This can be understood in two intuitively different ways. On the one conception, the particularized relation is a complex structure consisting of a relation and two particulars or relata – what is often called a "state of affairs." On the other conception, the relation as particularized is a sort of metaphysical "fundamental particle", with outward structural connections but no separable inner parts. Either way, the particularized relation, unlike a relation *simpliciter*, is not a repeatable as such; it is a one-off occurrence. As a succinct neutral term for particularized relations in these two senses, I adopt reluctantly Williams's word *trope*.[1] A trope, then, is a thing's having a property or the property as localized to that thing, or several things standing in relation or the relation of just those things. Whichever of the two intuitive conceptons of trope we adopt – complex structures or relative simples – the important thing about them for my purposes is what they can do, what structures they can form. To that architectonic end an inner structure is not essential. It is in this sense that the theory of tropes developed here exhibits them as basic: not as demonstrably ontologically ultimate or simple but as architectonic building blocks.

1A2   States of affairs

To know that London is in England is to know a trope, I said. We might have thought it was to know a *state of affairs*. What is the difference, if any? For many purposes, 'state of affairs' would be a convenient word to use in place of the more artificial 'trope'. But for many people 'state of affairs' seems irresistibly to suggest our first conception of trope, a relating in virtue of an inner structure. Since that is precisely the sense of 'trope' that I wish to soft-pedal (though not reject), it will be better not to use 'state of affairs' as a synonym. Instead, I shall reserve 'state of affairs' as a technical term for a set of possible worlds, what has often been called a "proposition". Every trope will then correspond to a "simple" state of affairs, the set of worlds where it exists. But not every state of affairs will correspond to a unique trope.

1A3   A world of tropes

Although I don't use 'state of affairs' interchangeably with 'trope', I do want to claim for tropes some of the things that have been said about states of affairs. Thus, according to Wittgenstein, "The world is the totality of facts, not of things" (1922: 1.1), where a fact is a state of affairs that obtains. If the world were different, different things would be the case, different states of affairs would obtain. Now, just as for Wittgenstein a world is given by the states of affairs that obtain in it, so I want to say that a world is given by the tropes that exist in it (as a first approximation).[2]

It might seem as though the world could also be different by containing different individual objects or events. But an individual exists, or enters into a world, I shall hold, through its tropes. Socrates exists only if Socrates' wisdom or Socrates' whiteness or what not exists. Thus a world without Socrates would differ from ours in its tropes, not just its objects. (Here I depart decidedly from Wittgenstein's doctrine of substance.) And an event, I hold, is just a particularly lively trope, as Williams notes (1953: 90).

The term "fact", as noted above, is usually applied to obtaining states of affairs, or sometimes to true propositions. I will use it to mean "existent trope".[3] This usage would not have pleased Williams:

> I shrink from endowing the theory of tropes with either the assets or the deficits of a theory of facts, of states of affairs, or of propositions. (1966: 91)

However, it enables me to agree verbally with Wittgenstein: the world is the totality of facts.

1A4   Relative criterion of individuation

Tropes, I said, are particularized properties and relations, particularized universals. Thus we have a criterion of individuation for tropes if we have one for universals (and for particulars), and perhaps vice versa. But individuating universals is notoriously problematic. How do we determine when coextensive properties are the same or different? Often on vague intuitive grounds, it would seem. The job is easier in particular cases. While it may not be immediately clear whether joy is the same property as happiness, it is a more manageable question whether Mary's joy now is the same fact or trope as Mary's happiness now. From the standpoint of individuation, then, tropes are prior to universals.

1A5   Tropes and universals

Thus the above informal explanation is not meant to imply that we start with universals as given and then particularize them, except heuristically. We never experience pure properties or relations without instances, any more than we encounter bare objects without properties and relations. What we come up against in the world are propertied and related objects, instantiated universals, wholes with both a particular side and a universal side; in a word, tropes. I take this epistemic priority to reflect a metaphysical priority. Instead of starting with the universal wisdom and whittling it down to fit Socrates, Aristotle, etc. as particular instances, trope theory starts with Socrates' wisdom, Aristotle's wisdom . . . and combines them to get wisdom. Thus wisdom is a bundle of tropes. The utility of this approach will emerge from the general theory that results. A criterion of adequancy for such a theory is that it explain and subsume the more familiar substance–attribute picture. Some may feel that a bundle lacks the over-arching unitary character that distinguished a universal (e.g. Campbell 1990: 12, 32, 62), but I shall continue to refer to properties and relations as "universals", even when construed as trope bundles. For such a bundle is a one over many, even if it isn't one atom fully and indivisibly shared by all its instances.

1A6   Ordinary names of tropes

Our language furnishes many ways of nominalizing a sentence. For example, 'Socrates is wise' gives rise to

> Socrates' wisdom
> Socrates' being wise
> that Socrates is wise

In various contexts all of these can be used to refer to a trope. The gerund phrase (with 'being') is probably least misleading, the 'that'-clause most confusing. The latter suggests to many people a state of affairs more strongly than the former. 'Socrates' wisdom' is a convenient abbreviation of the gerund phrase, but it is subject to a subtle ambiguity pointed out by Levinson (1980). It can mean either Socrates' property of being wise or the quality of Socrates' wisdom. The former assimilates more naturally to the 'that'-clause; only in the latter sense is a trope suggested. Thus we do best to stick to gerund phrases in English, using abstract forms like 'Socrates' wisdom' for short.

Whichever nominalization we use, however, it will derive from a sentence, with a subject and a predicate, suggesting that a trope is a composite structure consisting of a subject-like particular and a predicate-like universal. Thus ordinary language seems to favor a substance–attribute view of reality. It has no simple names of tropes. On reflection, this is not surprising. Words are useful as marking similarities and repetitions. A trope, just as such, never repeats. In adopting a trope ontology, we systematically resist the substance–attribute bias of ordinary language. While we shall occasionally refer to tropes by nominalized sentences, this carries no presumption of a subject-predicate-like structure in reality.

1A7   Pettit's problem

Suppose Dion is walking slowly; then, of course, he is walking. Dion's walking and Dion's walking slowly appear to be the same trope, and hence the same fact. Yet the fact that Dion is walking and the fact that Dion is walking slowly also appear to be different facts. This puzzle, pointed out to me by Philip Pettit,[4] is just the tip of an iceberg involving determinates and determinables, qualifying adjectives, and adverbs. We can begin to deal with this aspect of the problem by distinguishing two senses of 'fact': "existing trope" and "obtaining state of affairs" (cf. §1A2 above). Dion's walking and his walking slowly are the same existing trope but not the same obtaining state of affairs. This doesn't completely settle the matter, however. For in another possible world, Dion is walking fast. There, his walking seems to be identical not with his walking slowly but with his walking fast. The identity is accordingly contingent, but that raises another problem. I want to identify a possible world by its tropes (§1A3). Thus trope-identity is prior to world-identity, making identical tropes necessarily identical! We must recognize that, while 'Dion's walking' designates a trope, it doesn't designate it *rigidly*.[5] In the actual world (for the sake of the example) it designates Dion's walking slowly; in the other possible world it designates Dion's walking fast. The respective walkings need not even be the same trope. It is this nonrigidity that accounts for the contingent identity of Dion's walking with his walking slowly. Caution is accordingly indicated when we use ordinary gerund phrases to pick out tropes. If they aren't sufficiently determinate, the resulting nonrigidity can give rise to puzzles.

1A8 Tropes with instances?

As localized properties or particularized relations, tropes have their individual side. Helen's beauty has its Helen-aspect, for example, as well as its beauty-aspect. According to a variant of trope theory found by C. B. Martin (1980) in Locke (1689), by others in Reid (1895: 221, 376), considered favorably by D. M. Armstrong (1989b: 114, 116, 127), and adopted by Simons (1995), tropes are unsaturated thin properties (relations) still in need of individuals as instances. For me, Helen's beauty is a fact, an existing trope. On the Martin–Armstrong–Simons view, in contrast, Helen's beauty is a scrunched-up property that only yields a state of affairs when instantiated by Helen or some other individual. It might seem that Helen figures twice in the "state of affairs", first as the individuator of the beauty, and second as its instance. Here Martin and Armstrong part company. For Armstrong, Helen is not needed to individuate her beauty; it could just as well have been someone else's, say Phryne's. Tropes are *transferable*[6] from one individual to another. For Martin, on the other hand, Helen's beauty is essentially Helen's: it couldn't exist without *her* having it (cf. Armstrong 1989b: 117ff). Both versions of this view, which I call the *substance–trope view*, posit individuals as a separate basic category, instantiating the tropes. As I see it, on the other hand, individuals as a separate category are redundant. We can get everything we need in the way of individuals or particulars by taking them to be bundles of tropes. This does not settle the question of transferability, but it obviates any need for instances of tropes.

1A9 Beginning with tropes

I have introduced tropes as relatings, as particularized properties and relations. Whether the tropes are themselves made up of universals and particulars is left open, but no such inner structure is assumed. On the contrary, both universals and particulars will be constructed out of tropes, as will possible worlds. We begin to see the versatility of starting with tropes as our fundamental category.

1B Other Tropes?

1B1 Compound tropes?

As tropes of the sort so far considered correspond closely to simple states of affairs (§1A2), what about molecular states of affairs? Do they likewise correspond to a kind of trope, compound tropes? While Wittgenstein just takes it for granted (1922), a theory of compound states of affairs can indeed be developed, and it has some uses; cf. part 3D below. Van Fraassen (1975) and Cresswell (1973: 42ff) have pointed the way. It might seem natural enough to correlate these with "compound tropes", but it is not clear how. The states of affairs themselves, or the closely related n-tuples of §3D7, will serve just as well.[7] In any case, states of affairs (in my sense) are composed of tropes, which I want to treat as ontologically more basic. And simple tropes alone suffice for the semantic purpose of stating truth conditions for compound, complex, and general sentences of various sorts. Thus we have no need for compound tropes.

1B2 Nonexistent tropes

Facts, we said, are tropes that exist. This suggests that some tropes may fail to exist, such as Socrates' wealth or Thatcher's docility. Are there any such nonexistent tropes? Not in our world, but there might have been. Socrates' wealth is not a fact in the actual world. As the world is constituted by its facts, a world in which Socrates is rich will not be the actual world, but some other possible world. There Socrates' wealth will be a fact. Allowing nonexistent tropes thus gives us a way to conceive of possible worlds: a possible world is a set of tropes. This is a significant advantage, for something like possible worlds seems to be required for the semantics of intensional contexts and hence of natural language. The advantage is lost on *actualists*, to be sure, who recognize but one possible world, the actual one. They won't like nonexistent tropes either.[8] But actualists face a formidable task in accounting for modality. In particular, they have trouble with uninstantiated properties and with "alien" individuals, as I shall argue below (§§1D7, 4B2).[9]

1B3   Relational tropes

Among the tropes are relational ones involving two or more objects in relation. In shall call such polyadic tropes *polytropes*.[10] They are no more reducible to monadic tropes ("monotropes") than polyadic relations are reducible to monadic properties. Thus Dante's loving Beatrice is a dyadic trope. It isn't simply a matter of Dante's having some property and Beatrice's having some other, complementary property in some sort of pre-established harmony.[11] Notice that this is not the same dyadic trope as Beatrice's loving Dante. Thus a dyadic trope does not simply involve a relation and two terms: the order makes a difference, and similarly for *n*-adic tropes. It may well be wondered wherein this "order" consists *in rebus*, in the tropes, as opposed to the notational order distinguishing '*aRb*' from '*bRa*'.[12] Roughly, the idea is that Dante is involved in Dante's loving Beatrice from the same *aspect* as Beatrice is involved in Beatrice's loving Dante (if she does) or Sydney is involved in Sydney's being north of Wollongong. These "aspects" or facets corresponding to argument-places will be elucidated further in chapter 2, when we come to consider ways tropes can concur. While all polytropes are of finite degree, there is no evident upper bound to their degree. (Since we admit nonexistent tropes, it's not clear that it's just an empirical question, although it might be a question of scientific theory.)

1B4   Higher-level tropes

I take tropes to be metaphysically prior to objects and their properties and relations. In order to account for particulars and universals, however, we need certain sorting relations among tropes. To distinguish these from ground-level (0-level) relations of individuals, I shall call them first-level relations or *metarelations*.[13] There are three main metarelations: concurrence, likeness, and temporal precedence. The first two will be explained in more detail in part 1D. Here are some examples to illustrate them:

Dante's loving Beatrice

concurs with

Dante's writing *Il purgatorio*.

(They both have the same subject.[14]) It is like

Desdemona's loving Othello.

(They are both cases of the same relation.) Having rejected ground-level relations as ontologically basic, are we to accept metarelations as ultimate? We may not be forced to do so. Just as first-level tropes are metaphysically prior to ground-level relations, so we might recognize second-level tropes, or *hypertropes*, as metaphysically prior to metarelations. An example of such a hypertrope would be

Dante's loving Beatrice being like Desdemona's loving Othello.

The phrasing is a little confusing. Yet this hypertrope might be taken as metaphysically prior to the first-level trope, Dante's loving Beatrice, which in turn is prior to Dante, Beatrice, and love.

1B5 Infinite regress?

It may seem as though a regress threatens at this point. If there can be second-level tropes involving first-level tropes and metarelations, why not third-level tropes involving second-level tropes and *their* relations, and so on up? Such a hierarchy is not merely possible but of serious metaphysical interest. It turns out that no higher level is needed than a third or fourth. And the top-level relations needed to organize the tropes below form a simpler system than the three metarelations (cf. §5A3 below). The resulting picture is not very plausible, however. In the end, I shall take relations and metarelations as bundles but metametarelations (second-level relations) as basic.

1C   Metaphysical Construction

1C1   General theory of structure

With Williams, I take individual objects, properties, and relations to be metaphysical constructions out of tropes. By this I mean that objects and properties are made up of tropes, but not necessarily in the same way that armies are made up of soldiers or atoms of quarks. The quarks are physical components of the atom; the tropes are metaphysical components of the property. Unlike Russell, I do not want to deny that metaphysical constructions exist (1956a: 270ff). Physical structures and metaphysical structures both fall under the general theory of structure, which is set theory.

Together with logic and mathematics, I consider set theory to be the most fundamental part of philosophy.[15] It is prior to "first philosophy" or metaphysics, which draws on the theory of structure in positing the general kinds of structure that are best suited to explain the world as we find it. The elements of metaphysical structures are the concern of ontology, a comparatively trivial branch of metaphysics. The ontology of a metaphysical system surveys what sorts of items there are according to that metaphysic, and the conditions under which those items exist. As this inquiry will frequently lead back to questions of structure, ontology is parasitic upon metaphysics, even as a metaphysic is in a certain sese based upon its ontology.

1C2   Sets and ontology

Even at our best, we don't expect unanimity as to the right way to go about metaphysics. In the same way, we need not be unduly troubled by the lack of consensus as to the right system of set theory (or category theory or mereology). The modes of set-theoretic construction resorted to here intuitively and informally are available in most systems of set theory.

Although I use set theory as an ontological and metaphysical tool, it will be appropriate here to distance myself from certain metaphysical conceptions of set theory. The theory has been accused by some of ontological extravagance. If you can slap just about any things together into a set or class, you will be multiplying "entities" beyond necessity. Already the sequence Λ, $\{\Lambda\}$, $\{\{\Lambda\}\}$, . . . is infinite, and its power set more infinite still. Well, my view is that Λ and $\{\Lambda\}$ are two different things, $\Lambda \neq \{\Lambda\}$, and so *ad infinitum*, but I didn't create that infinity by espousing set theory. Rather, that infinity makes part of set theory true. Does this mean that I count Λ, $\{\Lambda\}$, etc. as existents, as part of my ontology? I tend to think so, but not every set exists, nor does every member of every set. For example, a merely possible world is a nonexistent (inactual) set of tropes, some of which may themselves fail to exist.[16]

1C3   Sets and everyday objects

To some thinkers it appears obvious that concrete, everyday objects are not sets or classes, the latter being "abstract". To take an extreme case, many will take it for granted that Madonna, flesh-and-blood creature that she is, with throbbing heart and perhaps immortal soul, is not just a *set*! For metaphysical purposes, I don't find this a very fruitful stricture. If Madonna is complex and has a certain make-up, then she has a structure. The general theory of structure applies. Of course, it may be beyond our powers to say what set she is, just as it's beyond our powers to say what physical structure she is, even granting physicalism. Similar remarks apply to more everyday structures than Madonna.[17]

1C4   Atoms

Thus far I have used the terms 'simple' and 'basic' in a relative or comparative sense. First-level tropes are more basic metaphysically than universals. If an item is basic to others, while none is more basic, that item is an ultimate metaphysical constituent, an "*atom*". From the above account of structure, it will be clear that atoms are what are usually called "individuals" or "Urelemente" in set theory (though not in trope theory), i.e. non-sets. (Perhaps the empty set should also be accounted an atom, i.e. a memberless item.) Atoms, if there are any, are central to ontology.

The term 'atom' derives, of course, from Russell's (1918): his "atomism" was "logical" in the sense of 'set-theoretic'. But I don't accept Russell's influential view that atoms "have a kind of reality not belonging to anything else" (1956a: 270), and that all sets and therefore all metaphysical structures are mere "logical fictions" (1956a: 272). (For a helpful discussion of Russell's logical atomism, see Lycan 1979.)

1C5   Are there any?

Do we have any reason to believe that there are atoms? Armstrong has argued eloquently that we don't (1978b: 32ff). Atomisms, he charges, tend to read ontological simplicity into our need for semantic and epistemological simplicity. (Infinitely complex structures, it may be thought, could mean nothing to us and could not be known by us. But actually, both mathematics and linguistics seem to furnish counterexamples to this supposition.) I suggest that we do have reason to believe in atoms: the methodological canon of explanatory simplicity as a working hypothesis. Although this is reminiscent of the specious epistemological argument rightly disparaged by Armstrong, it is not an argument purporting to establish atomism as a conclusion. It merely declares that of two proposed competing metaphysical theories, other things being equal, the presumption is in favor of the atomistic one, and it encourages us to try to come up with such a theory. More controversial working hypotheses are widely accepted by contemporary philosophers, such as physicalism.

1C6   Indeterminacy of atoms

A further problem posed by the search for atoms is that it's possible to construct isomorphic structures X and Y such that the atoms or unanalyzed basic objects of X correspond to structured complexes of Y and vice versa. It's rather like the interdefinability of truth-functional connectives: given negation, disjunction can be defined in terms of conjunction and vice versa. Which, then, is more basic? In the case of structures, overall theoretical simplicity must decide. But it is not in general guaranteed that there will be such a basis for choice.

1D   Universals

1D1   Similarities and bundles

The theory of tropes accounts for individuals as well as their properties and relations by means of bundles of tropes.[18] A *bundle* is a similarity class – a maximal set of tropes all similar to each other. It is *maximal* in that nothing similar to all the members is left out. 'Similarity' is used here as a placeholder for various reflexive and symmetric relations – *similarity relations*.[19] Bundles can overlap, but one bundle can never be wholly included in another. For suppose the contrary: two bundles X and Y such that $X \subset Y$; and let an arbitrary $x \in Y$. Then x is similar to all members of Y and therefore to all members of X. So by maximality $x \in X$. That establishes $Y \subseteq X$, making $X = Y$, contrary to our supposition.[20]

Non-overlapping bundles will be called *tight* bundles. They arise when the similarity relation is also *transitive*. Transitive similarity relations are called *equivalence relations*; tight bundles are commonly called *equivalence classes*.[21]

1D2   Likeness

Of the three metarelations, or relations between tropes, two are similarity relations, concurrence and likeness. *Like* tropes are (circularly) ones that are to involve the same property or relation, for example Socrates' wisdom and Aristotle's wisdom. These are like tropes in that both are cases of the same property, both are wisdoms. Phryne's beauty and Helen's beauty are like tropes, twin beauties (in the abstract sense). I'm using Campbell's term 'likeness' (1990: 35) here in place of Williams's 'precise similarity' (1966: 80).[22] It will sometimes be symbolized by 'H' (for 'horizontal similarity'). It's important to recognize that although I've referred to properties in this explanation of likeness, the likeness is metaphysically prior to the properties.

1D3   Simple universals

As a similarity relation, likeness sorts its field, the tropes, into similarity classes or bundles. These bundles can do the work of simple universals – properties and relations. Thus, for example, the property of wisdom is the set of all the wisdoms:

wisdom = {Socrates' wisdom, Aristotle's wisdom, . . .},

and similarly for relations of various degrees.

According to Campbell, a property in trope theory "is not a universal but a collection of tropes" (1990: 32). "It is precisely . . . the complete presence of the universal in every one of its different exemplars, which is the critical, and fatal, distinguishing mark of the real universal" (1990: 62). Campbell's position differs only verbally from mine in this regard. In my terminology, that a thing is a class does not disqualify it from existing or being a universal. (Cf. §1D10 below.)

1D4   Is likeness transitive?

According to Williams,

> speaking roughly again, the set or sum of tropes precisely similar to a given trope . . . may be supposed to be, or at least to correspond formally to, the abstract universal . . . which it may be said to exemplify. (1953: 80)

This strongly suggests, although it does not actually imply, that likeness is transitive.[23] Otherwise the possibility would be left open that one of the tropes might be like the given trope but not like the others. For example, an orangeness trope might be like the color of a given tomato, which in turn was like a bunch of redness tropes. The tomato's color might be both an orangeness and a redness. Yet the orangeness trope might *not* be like any of the other redness tropes.[24] I see no compelling reason to exclude such possibilities a priori. If we did, likeness would become transitive and its bundles tight (non-overlapping).

That would be architectonically convenient, and is in fact assumed in some trope theories. But notice what would happen to colors in that case. Every color trope would have to be assigned to a unique color; tropes of different colors could never be alike. The result would be many, many very narrow colors, among which ordinary redness, blueness, etc. would not be found. The latter could then be accommodated as disjunctions (cf. §1D8). This ploy seems artificial, however. I prefer to allow properties to overlap and likeness to be nontransitive.

This will have the unexpected advantage of allowing us to treat certain adverbs and qualifying adjectives as denoting properties. For example, bigness (denoted by the qualifying adjective – not predicate – 'big') will be a loose bundle partially overlapping mousehood, manhood, etc. (cf. §3A9 below).

1D5   Companionship

Contemplating Dion's promenade (§1A7), we observed that slow walkings are walkings, though not necessarily vice versa. In Carnap's terms, walking is a *companion* (*Begleiter*) of slow walking. Yet if both are properties, likeness bundles, that means that the one bundle will be wholly included in the other. Such inclusion is incompatible with likeness's being a similarity relation (§1D1). If all the walkings are alike, the slow walkings will not form a bundle. The set of slow walkings will not be *maximal*: some tropes that are like all its members will be missing. This is a variant of Carnap's companionship problem (1928: §70), grappled with also by Goodman (1951: ch. 5). If slow walkings are reckoned as tropes of walking, then walking but not slow walking will emerge as a simple property. Slow walking will be a derivative property involving adverbial modification (cf. §3A9 below). The alternative would be to make walking slowly a simple property but not walking. Carried to its logical extreme, such an approach would recognize only properties that were maximally modified adverbially, as it were, which seems unwieldy. We shall, however, see that only such properties – "syntropic" properties, as I call them – can individuate tropes (§§1E4, ch. 5 n. 8).

1D6   Determinates and determinables

It would appear that redness is to color as slow walking is to walking. I have suggested that walking, not slow walking, is the simple or basic property. Shall we analogously admit color(edness) but not redness as a simple property? The suggestion sounds fantastic. After all, isn't every color trope either a redness trope or an organeness trope or what not?

We have two interesting alternatives, neither entirely satisfactory. If we take coloredness as the simple property, then the determinates, redness, blueness, etc., will presumably be something like subproperties in the sense of §3A9: "redly colored", "bluely colored", etc. And if no color trope is both a redness and a blueness – i.e., no coloredness is both a being colored redly and a being colored bluely – then it will follow with the help of syntropy (§1E4) that no individual can be both red and blue. Color incompatibility will receive that much explanation. It will also fall out naturally that everything red is colored.

If, on the other hand, we take the various colors as simple properties, and their embodiments as tropes, there will be nothing in our scheme as so far developed to prevent an individual from being both red and blue. Such a restriction would have to be added in its own right, like a meaning postulate. The incompatibility would remain unexplained. And coloredness would be an indefinitely long disjunction, perhaps in principle unspecifiable. Here I have a slight preference for the second alternative, but the first one actually seems to have more to recommend it. It's just that redness feels intuitively more basic than color.

1D7 Empty properties

Are there properties (and relations) that nothing has? Armstrong has argued that there are not (1978a: 113(1); 1978b: 9f, 76ff). One motive may be that it's natural to deny the existence of uninstantiated properties. 'There's no such thing as clairvoyance, neurasthenia, or teleportation,' we're inclined to say, meaning 'Nothing (nobody) is clairvoyant, nobody is neurasthenic, nothing is teleported.' But if it's possible that somebody might be clairvoyant, then clairvoyance is possible: it's instantiated and hence exists in some possible world. To exist in a world is to be instantiated there. So there are some properties that are empty and don't *exist* in the actual world, but *do* exist in some possible world. Such properties are bundles of exclusively nonexistent (in this world) tropes. Without nonexistent tropes we could not make sense of possible but actually empty properties (cf. §1B2). And without nonexistent tropes we could never distinguish two such properties: both would be the empty bundle.[25] In a modal context, to be sure – admitting nonexistent tropes and possible worlds – the empty bundle would be *the* one impossible property. Later, however, properties will be allowed to vary from world to world, permitting more than one empty property, or attribute, in a given world (§7A7).

1D8 Degrees of likeness?

Williams follows the passage quoted at the beginning of §1D4 with this aside:

> The tropes approximately similar to the given one provide a less definite universal. (1953: 81)

Perhaps developing this point, Campbell writes

> The closeness of resemblance between the tropes in a set can vary. These variations correspond to the different degrees to which different properties are specific. (1981: 484)

Varying closeness of resemblance; approximate rather than precise similarity – these would be *additional* metarelations, whose similarity bundles would form whole crisscrossing sets of progressively less specific universals. Campbell suggests that this is the way to deal with determinable–determinate or genus–species relations. The cost is high. The more primitive metarelations we admit into trope theory, the closer it gets to a substance–attribute conception in its baroqueness. Conceivably there could be other uses as well for such a scheme. Until I have seen what they are, though, I shall rest content with a single likeness relation. I have shown elsewhere that one such relation suffices for the semantics of quantified modal logic, with its rather complex panoply of properties and relations (Bacon 1988). Perhaps it will suffice for other purposes as well.

1D9   Compound universals

Just as we can make sense of the idea of compound states of affairs (§1B1; 3D), so we may recognize compound or derivative universals. Rather than assemble them out of compound states of affairs, however, in analogy to the universals already introduced, we can *construct* compound universals directly out of *simple* ones, suitably adapted. The details are deferred to chapter 3. The most straightforward way of compounding properties may be mentioned here, however, by way of example. It is not conjunction, as we might have expected, but *disjunction*. The disjunction of two properties is just their union. Conjunction and negation are more complicated.

1D10   Theory of universals

D. M. Armstrong has done much to restore the theory of universals to its rightful place in philosophy. No longer need it cry, in the words Kant quoted, *"modo maxima rerum, tot generis natisque potens . . . nunc trahor exul, inops"* (Kant 1781: p. ix; Ovid 1916: book XIII, ll. 508ff). On Armstrong's approach, a central part of the theory is the doctrine of compound properties – cf. my

1986 essay. In that spirit, our construction of compound properties is the beginning of a theory of universals based on trope-bundle theory.

This claim stands, notwithstanding its "loose language", as Campbell would have it: "Except in the loosest of languages, Resemblance theories are not theories of *universals*" (1990: 32). Universals are "items that can be literally fully shared by indefinitely many objects. A Universal can be in many places at once *without being divided*" (1990: 12). Depending on how we take 'fully shared' and 'divided', this definition strongly suggests that "universals" must be simple or ontologically basic. Although the dispute is ultimately merely verbal, I reject Campbell's requirement. As I approach universals, that is to say properties and relations of various kinds, they manifest themselves to us in a certain structure. It is the job of a theory of universals to account for that structure and perhaps to tidy it up a bit. This leaves open in the first instance whether universals are best accounted atoms or complexes of some sort (cf. §1D3).

1E Individuals

1E1 Terminology

Things of the sort that may be said to exemplify the properties just considered are often called "individuals" in logic and "particulars" in metaphysics; in German, *'Objekt'* is often used. The trouble with 'particular', the obvious correlative of 'universal', is that since Stout *tropes* have often been called "abstract particulars". Compare Armstrong: "Admit properties and relations, *but make them into particulars*", i.e. tropes (1989b: 16). In logic, 'individual' is well entrenched. But it suggests the result of individuation, and universals and items of other sorts may also be individuated. In shall use 'individual' and 'particular' interchangeably, with a preference for 'individual'. There is no presumption that "individuals" in the set- or type-theoretic sense are meant, or atoms or substances. (The terms 'thing' and 'item' I reserve for wider uses. There is a sense in which it is natural to reckon individuals as "0-level" or "ground-level tropes"; cf. ch. 1 n. 13.)

1E2   Concurrence

Two tropes *concur*, according to Williams, when they both involve the same individual. (This way of putting it inverts the intended priority of tropes over individuals.) Thus Socrates' wisdom concurs with Socrates' whiteness, in that both are states of the same individual. Concurrence, for short I, in this simple, straightforward sense is limited to monadic tropes. For polyadic tropes a more complicated relation of aspectual concurrence (concurrence in the ith argument-place) will be needed, which in turn complicates the structure of individuals. I leave this fuller conception of individual aside until the next chapter. Here I shall take up only the limiting case in which all tropes are monadic and hence all universals are properties.

1E3   Individuals

Concurrence is an equivalence relation. Thus it partitions mono-tropes into tight bundles, our first approximation of concrete particulars or individuals. (For technical reasons, these will sometimes be called "proto-particulars" to acknowledge the neglect of relational tropes, but I won't bother here.) The bundles are tight because a monotrope as explained involves just one individual; hence it should belong to just one bundle. (For the contrary view, see Bacon 1989: §31).

Individuals and properties are thus on this approach things of the same kind: bundles of tropes. Williams, to be sure, leaned toward taking a concrete particular to be the mereological fusion of its bundle (1953: 81), but that becomes too crude structurally when we move on to polytropes and relations. (See also §§3C1–3C4 below.) On my approach, it can even happen that one and the same bundle is both an individual and a property. An example might be {God's divinity} on the monotheistic conception. Such a singleton property-individual is unlikely, however, in view of the following two constraints on the metarelations H and I.

1E4 Syntropy

A monadic trope is often uniquely determined by the individual and the property it involves. Such a property will be called a *syntropic* property. For example, the *Rh*− blood type is a syntropic property. There is just one way for a person (or a blood sample) to have it. Armstrong rejects nonsyntropic properties and argues that trope theory can do so only by posing an *ad hoc* restriction (1978a: 86). Campbell rejects nonsyntropic properties for the most part on Ockhamist grounds (1990: 66ff). Nevertheless, I want to leave the door open to nonsyntropic properties. Typically, they are properties whose predicates admit of adverbial modification, such as walking: walking slowly, walking fast. Walking is not syntropic: there is not just one way for Dion to walk. His walking is not a unique trope. Of course, in this world it is; syntropy fails only when nonexistent tropes in other possible worlds are taken into account. (Since Campbell and Armstrong don't recognize nonexistent tropes, this is not a disagreement with them about syntropy or multiple instances in the actual world.) Syntropy is of interest as a prerequisite for property negation (§3A3).

1E5 Plenitude

I assume further that each individual overlaps each syntropic property (and hence each property) by at least one common trope. This assumption I call *plenitude*. It is required only for the sake of negative universals in a context of multiple possible worlds; otherwise it may want plausibility. Together, syntropy and plenitude guarantee that any individual and any syntropic property will share a unique trope (though it may not exist in the actual world).

1E6 Possible worlds revisited

A possible world, we said (§1B2), is a set of tropes, those existing in that world. This is a natural extension of the Wittgensteinian conception of *the* world with which we began, as Skyrms has pointed out (1989). It is echoed by Williams:

> Any possible world, and hence, of course, this one, is completely constituted by its tropes and their connections of location and similarity, and any others there may be. (1953: 80)

Alter the tropes and you alter the possible world. Williams' statement further suggests, though, that different possible worlds might be formed by varying the metarelations of concurrence and likeness. In fact, Williams (1953: 79), Armstrong (1989b: 126) and Campbell (1990: 31ff) all take likeness to be an *internal* relation, and hence the same for all possible worlds in which its terms exist. Concurrence, on the other hand, they take to be *external*, varying from world to world (e.g. Campbell 1990: 132ff). Here I shall assume for convenience for the time being that concurence too is internal: two tropes just concur or don't concur, regardless of world. This assumption is analogous to one often made in the model theory of quantified modal logic, the assumption of a constant domain of individuals for all worlds. Both assumptions are questionable and probably untenable in the end (cf. chapter 4 below), but they will smooth our way into the problem.

All the same, there is a sense in which our concurrence and likeness already vary from world to world; namely, their subrelations as restricted to (tropes existing in) different worlds will not in general be the same.[27]

1E7   Simple instantiation

The two-story substance–attribute picture of reality takes instantiation or exemplification as a primitive relation or "nonrelational tie" connecting the two stories. Trope theory provides an explication of instantiation ("to dispel the ancient mystery of predication", in Williams' wry phrase (1953: 82). In semantic terms, this would mean giving truth conditions for simple sentences in terms of trope-bundles.

At the ground level (monadic tropes, simple properties, tight bundles as individuals), instantiation is *overlapping*, non-empty intersection, symbolized here as '$\bigcirc$' (i.e., $X \bigcirc Y =_{df} X \cap Y \neq \Lambda$). Socrates has wisdom, Socrates is wise in world w, if and only if Socrates and wisdom jointly overlap w:

Socrates is wise in w iff Socrates $\cap$ wisdom $\bigcirc$ w.

This will hold, e.g., if

Socrates = {Socrates' whiteness, Socrates' wisdom, . . .}
wisdom = {Socrates' wisdom, Aristotle's wisdom, . . .}, and
w = {Socrates' whiteness, Socrates' wisdom, Aristotle's wisdom, Chicago's largeness, . . .}

They all share a trope, namely Socrates' wisdom. If this looks circular, remember that while 'Socrates' wisdom' is a complex expression in our language, it stands for a simple trope in the theory. Thus an individual instantiates a property in w iff all three overlap.

It will be noticed that this account is in a certain sense symmetric as between individuals and properties. We might almost as well say that the property instantiates the individual. This reflection is reminiscent of Ramsey's challenge to show what distinguishes particulars from universals (1931), as D. H. Mellor has pointed out to me. What distinguishes them on our scheme are the different metarelations that generate them. Simple instantiation is by definition a relation whose domain is I-equivalence classes and whose codomain is H-similarity classes. We could turn it around into a definition of the converse, application, but that would not make individuals into universals or vice versa. (By analogy, a bedroom and a bathroom are ensuite if they share a wall and a door. Although the sharing is a symmetric relation, this doesn't make the bathroom a bedroom or vice versa.)

With some frills, the spirit of this explication of instantiation can be preserved as we move from simple to compound properties (cf. §1D9 and chapter 3).[28]

1E8   Existence

This account of instantiation leads naturally to an analysis of existence, both singular and general. Where X is any bundle, whether individual (proto-particular) or universal, to say that X *exists* in world w is just to say that X overlaps w:

$$E_w X \text{ iff } X \bigcirc w.$$

When X is a property, this is as much as to say that X is instantiated in w; cf. §1D7. When X is an individual, it will say that X has some property in w. Thus in one fell swoop we get accounts of both general and singular existence that are already familiar in the literature. (Being instantiated was Frege's account of general existence, formalized in his invention of the existential quantifier (1879: §11). Having a property was consider by Leonard as a candidate for an explication of singular existence, recalling the *cogito* (1956: 56).) I wouldn't want to claim E_w as the only tenable conception of existence. Indeed, it seems likely that 'exists' is a term of art imbued with whatever meaning it has by the theoretical context. (It seems also to have an everyday use, which is not easy to pin down.) But I do think this analysis is a useful one, if not for McX's, then perhaps for some Wymans (Zedskys?).

1E9   Prospectus

The basic framework of a metaphysic of tropes has now been sketched. I have explained the basic ideas and themes in some detail, acknowledged their paternity, and related them to the work of contemporary metaphysicians. Much remains to be worked out. Individuals must be complicated still further to account for relational instantiation (chapter 2). The theory of compound universals will be extended to cover conjunction, negation, and relations (3Aff.). The simple states of affairs corresponding to tropes will be explicated as sets of possible worlds, which in turn lend themselves to compounding (3D). And what about compound individuals (3C)?

Problems of intensionality and transworld individuation ultimately force us to complicate possible worlds (4A; 7A7f) along the lines anticipated in §1E6. The resulting construction of possible worlds can still be viewed as "combinatorial", but not as actualist: "alien" tropes must be admitted (4B), as foreshadowed in §1B2. On such a basis the various alethic modalities can be sorted out afresh (§4C). Following Russell's lead (1914: chapter 4), common-sense time is reconstructed out of a before-and-after relation between temporal tropes (chapter 6 below). Finally, I consider carefully the status of the metarelations and accessibility relations required for trope theory (chapter 5). A reduction to third- or fourth-level tropes, as suggested in §1B5, is ultimately rejected as unhelpful. I conclude that the requisite relations are real and basic to trope theory, which is a little simpler than its rivals all the same.

Williams wrote, "A philosophy of tropes calls for completion in a dozen directions at once" (1953: 84). A couple of those directions are pursued here. Foremost among them is the analysis of belief. It is characterized by a tetradic accessibility relation. The objects of belief, "propositions", are construed as functions from worlds to states of affairs (chapter 7). Although such a treatment is possible without the trope basis, it comes across as particularly natural in this context.

States of affairs, or sets of possible worlds, are suited to act as causes and effects. This comes out particularly in referentially opaque causal contexts. David Lewis's theory of causation 1973b, based on counterfactual dependence, is adapted to propositions in my sense, taking account also of relevance (chapter 8). As bearers of inherent value, tropes give rise to a relation of comparative value of possible worlds, in terms of which duty can be defined (chapter 9).

It thus emerges that many strands of first philosophy can be spun out of tropes.

2

Relational Tropes and Individuals

2A Relations of Individuals in Trope Theory

2A1 What are the relata?

Logic accustoms us to regard relations as higher-degree properties, properties with extra argument places. This suggests that trope theory should be able to treat relations of individuals in the same way as properties of individuals. Socrates' wisdom is a monotrope belonging to the monadic property wisdom. Likewise, Socrates' teaching Plato is a dyadic trope belonging to the dyadic relation of teaching. The monotrope is a "thin" or particularized property, the dyadic trope a "thin" or particularized relation. So far trope theorists more or less agree. But their views diverge as to the *terms* of such relations. And this divergence is reflected in their conceptions of the relations themselves.

Here as elsewhere the exposition of trope theory is somewhat hampered by the substance–attribute bias of our natural language. It appears obvious that relations of individuals have individuals as their terms. But what do we take as the "individuals": atoms (§1C4), such as tropes; ordinary objects; or objects reconstrued as bundles? Campbell considers the first and third options; Armstrong and I take the second option; and the third is ascribed to Stout and Williams by Armstrong (1989b: 114).

2A2 Tropes as relata? Campbell

All trope theorists agree that the metarelations of concurrence and likeness relate tropes. But what about ground-level relations of individuals? According to Campbell, these too really relate tropes: "the only items available to be the terms of any relation are themselves tropes" (1990: 98ff); "in a metaphysic that makes first-order tropes the terms of all relations, relational tropes must belong to a second, derivative order" (1981: 487). Thus what I have called ground-level relations, prima facie relations of individuals, are construed by Campbell as first-level relations, relations of tropes. Like ground-level properties, these first-level relations break down into instances, tropes, in this case second-level relational tropes. (On my use of '-level', which diverges from Campbell's '-order', see ch. 1 n. 13.) But, very oddly, "Monadic tropes require no bearer, polyadic ones call for at least two, which will have to be themselves tropes" (1990: 99).

Thus, at the level of relations, Campbell seems implicitly to forsake the one-category conception that has informed his treatment of tropes thus far for the substance–trope conception of Martin (1980) and Simons (1995), commended by Armstrong (1989b: 116, 127). "It is at least a plausible thesis," contends Campbell, "that a world in which there are neither substances nor monadic qualities but there are nevertheless relations [i.e., relational tropes], is impossible" (1990: 98);[1] "the trope philosophy cannot treat qualities and relations as differing only in the number of their bearers" (1990: 99). Yet Campbell does not in fact think of himself as espousing the Locke–Martin view at the relational level:

> Using the image of God's creative activity, . . . since God must deal with the terms one by one, to give them individuality and their monadic properties, might He not be able to complete the job, relations and all, dealing with the terms singly rather than in pairs? (1990: 99)

Relations are not needed as a distinct ontological category. They are held to supervene on monadic properties.

Often Campbell nevertheless speaks of the "terms" of a relation as though its ordinary terms were meant, individuals or bundles. As near as I can make it out, his foundationism comes to this. A relation-trope, a's bearing R to b, is no ontic addition to, but supervenes upon, the monadic tropes making up the individuals a and b. Some of these monadic tropes are the foundations of the relation-trope. If I've got this right, it could tempt us to think that the relation, ostensibly relating individuals, "really" relates the foundations, i.e. monadic tropes. That could explain Campbell's assertion that the terms must be tropes. Actually, though, I don't think it is in the spirit of Campbell's treatment to make the foundations the relata, for that would threaten a regress as in his discussion of Russell (1990: 103). That leaves individual bundles as the relata. This is how Armstrong reads Campbell: "Particulars *reduce* to bundles of compresent tropes. Relation-tropes can then relate such bundles" (1989b: 114).

2A3 Independence of relata

Why does Campbell reject the parallelism between properties and relations that has proved so serviceable in modern logic? "No relations can exist (or be instantiated) except where all their terms do. No terms, no relations" (1990: 98). But in this regard monadic properties are no different from relations. A property may be empty, uninstantiated in the actual world. But where a property exists, in the sense of being instantiated, its subject must also exist. The subject exists not as a bearer or substrate but as a bundle of concurring tropes intersecting the property in question in the actual world. None of this militates against the ontological simplicity of the trope(s) in the intersection. Such a trope may exist independently, yet in virtue of that trope its property is instantiated and its subject exists. From the fact that relations require terms, it doesn't follow that they require pre-existing terms.

2A4 Tropes as bundles

If, with Campbell and me (§1B4), one recognizes second-level tropes, presumably they can also concur with and be like one another. The resulting bundles should be first-level tropes and relations. (I carry out just such a construction in 1989: §14; cf. §5A3 below.) Far from assuming first-level tropes as the necessary pre-existing bearers of relations or relation tropes, we can get the former out of the latter. I don't say that such a construction is forced upon us, but it would be in the spirit of trope theory.

2A5   Supervenience and natures

Campbell's thesis that relations supervene on monadic properties turns out to be equivalent to the identity of property-indiscernibles, provided that identity is counted as a relation. For if relations thus supervene, then so will identity. Hence objects with just the same monadic properties will be identical with just the same things and so with each other. Conversely, if objects with the same monadic properties are identical, then by the indiscernibility of identicals they will stand in just the same relations.

The identity of property-indiscernibles is not easily refuted, but it is a controversial assumption. It boils down to the claim that each individual is uniquely characterized by the conjunction of its properties, which we might call its "nature". Given natures, we could construct relations. The construction can be read off the representation of a relation as a set of n-tuples. (This is not how I take ground-level relations, but it makes the point.) For example, let $R^2 = \{\langle a, b \rangle, \langle b, b \rangle, \langle c, a \rangle\}$, and let A, B, C be the natures of a, b, c respectively. Then xR^2y just in case Ax & By ∨ Bx & By ∨ Cx & Ay, and $R^2 = A \times B \cup B \times B \cup C \times A$. (An infinite relation becomes an infinite union, incapable of being written out.)[2] Thus Campbell's supervenience of relations upon properties is actually the reducibility of relations to natures.

But is there any good reason to believe in such natures? On the contrary, irreducible relations are equally constitutive of most objects. Twin cars, sharing all monadic properties, might conceivably roll off a particularly well-honed Japanese assembly line: only their relational properties would distinguish them. If, as Aristotle sensibly held, men and women are essentially social, then relations to others will be part of their natures. Even when every relational difference answers to a property-difference, it need not be necessarily so, as supervenience would require. So trope theory ought to provide a place for real ground-level relations, not merely supervenient ones.

2A6   Parallelism restored

In order to allow for the possibility that relations enter into the natures of particulars or individuals, we must restore the parallelism between ground-level relations and properties. Both characterize individuals. As Armstrong says, "Relation-tropes are relations holding between particulars" (1989b: 116). Such ground-level relations are to be sharply distinguished from first-level relations or metarelations between tropes, such as concurrence and likeness. The parallel between relations and properties turns out to complicate the structure of the individual, as we shall see below. As a compensation, relations relations the simplicity of properties.

2B   Bundles of Polytropes

2B1   Relations as bundles

In chapter 1, simple universals were recognized as bundles of like tropes (§1D2). Among such universals are ground-level relations of various degrees. The degree of a relation is given by the degree of its member tropes, which must be uniform. In other words, like tropes have like degree. If their degree is greater than one, the relation is polyadic and the tropes are polytropes (cf. §1B3). A monadic relation or universal is, as before, a property.

Apart from relations of individuals, it does not appear possible to construe all the relations needed in trope theory as bundles. It is possible for the metarelations, as Williams anticipated (1953: 84) – cf. §1B5 above. But some irreducible relations in the ordinary or set-theoretic sense will always be presupposed. In (1989) I introduced the term 'protorelation' to distinguish polytrope bundles from relations in the set-theoretic sense, i.e. sets of n-

tuples. Here I shall just use 'relation' for both; which is meant should be sufficiently clear from the context.[3] The bundles are our present concern.

2B2   Concurrence of polytropes

So likeness gives rise to polyadic relations as well as to properties. The existence of polytropes poses no special problem for universals, including relations. But it does complicate the preliminary account of individuals given in chapter 1. Individuals (protoparticulars) were there construed as tight bundles of concurring tropes, concurrence equivalence classes (§1E3). Two tropes concur, intuitively, when they involve the same individual (cf. §1E2). But consider the two tropes:

(1)   Othello's loving Desdemona
(2)   Iago's hating Othello

Both involve Othello, but they involve him in different ways: (1) as "subject"; (2) as "object". Do the two tropes concur? If they did, (2) would also concur with:

(3)   Cassio's trusting Iago

Concurrence being transitive, that would mean that (1) concurred with (3). Yet (1) and (3) have no individual in common. More serious problems arise when we try to extend our account of simple instantiation (§1E7) to relations.

2B3   Aspectual concurrence

The solution is to relativize concurrence to argument-places. Thus we can say that

(4)   Othello's trusting Iago

concurs with (1) in the first argument-place (or subject position) and with (3) in the second argument-place (or object position).

But this talk of argument-places is linguistic: it's the phrases that have argument-places or subject positions. Let us call the corresponding features of the tropes "aspects" (cf. §1B3). We may think of these as numbered, like the argument-places, although there is nothing inherent in the trope that gives its "first" aspect priority over its "second" aspect. (As an analogy, two people may have the same size of no. 8 tooth and different sizes of no. 5 teeth, but the numbering is an arbitrary convention of dentistry.) Let us say, then, that (4) concurs with (1) in its first aspect, or that they *1-concur*. Similarly, (3) and (4) *2-concur*. But now what about (4) and

(5)   Iago's being trusted by Othello?

These seem to be the same trope; does it 1-concur with (1) or (2)? Does it 2-concur with (3) or (2)? It's obviously arbitrary, like the numbering above. The important thing is that *some* order of aspects be laid down and consistently maintained. Whether that order is metaphysically rooted may be beyond our ken.

We shall have, then, as many different aspectual concurrence relations as tropes can have aspects, perhaps infinitely many. For each i, i-concurrence, for short I^i, is a similarity relation: thus it sorts the tropes into loose bundles or similarity classes, called *i-bundles*. Although the I^is, considered thus as dyadic, may be infinite in number, they could all be regarded as instances of a single triadic metarelation I between the aspect i and two tropes, provided that weren't taken as reifying i.

2B4   Right-inflation

In order for i-concurrence to be a similarity relation between tropes, it must assign each trope to an i-bundle. What about tropes with fewer than i aspects? It might seem most natural to exclude these from the field of i-concurrence. Or we might group them all into the same i-bundle, or take each one's singleton as its own separate i-bundle. The resulting degenerate i-bundles would be of little use in representing individuals, however. A more fruitful approach is suggested by predicate-functor logic: let each less than i-adic trope belong to *all* i-bundles. In fact, it is only these degenerate i-concurrents that prevent i-bundles from being tight or equivalence classes. Otherwise, as applied to at least i-adic tropes, I^i is transitive. Call this convention *right-inflation*. Although somewhat artificial and not forced upon us, right-inflation will simplify our account of relational and compound universals.

2B5   Bundle-chains

We are now in a position to extend the preliminary conception of individuals, or proto-particulars, developed in the context of monadic tropes in §1E3. Instead of being just a concurrence bundle, an individual will now be a whole set of i-bundles for $i = 1, 2, \ldots$ As in general there is no upper bound on i, the set may be infinite. Such a set of bundles will be called a *bundle-chain*; individuals are bundle-chains. Each bundle in the chain is a different facet of the individual, so to speak. Where a is such a particular, we may refer to its i-bundle as a^i; thus $a = \langle a^1, a^2, \ldots \rangle$.[4] Intuitively a^1 is the set of all tropes involving a in their first aspect, a^2 the tropes with a in their second aspect, and so on.

2B6   Collimation

Bundle-chains should clearly not cross anywhere. (Otherwise it might happen that, say, $\text{Mary}^2 = \text{Sue}^2$, so that whoever loved Mary would also love Sue and vice versa. But we want to leave open possible worlds in which John loves only Mary, not Sue, etc.) Thus bundle-chains are *collimated*, carded out into discrete lines, as it were. In other words, $a^i = b^i$ for no i unless $a = b$:

$$a^i = b^i \rightarrow a = b.$$

Collimation is a basic constraint on i-concurrence.

One way of securing it automatically is to assume a universal n-adic relation, say

$$\Xi^n = \hat{x}_1 \ldots \hat{x}_n (x_1 = x_1 \ \& \ldots \& \ x_n = x_n),[5]$$

for the highest n. (If there is none, this won't work.) Then the trope corresponding to $\Xi^n a \ldots a^{(n)}$ will be in a^1 iff it is in a^i. Thus if $a^i = b^i$, they will share the trope $\Xi^n a \ldots a^{(n)}$, as will a^1 and b^1 and in fact a^j and b^j for all $j \leq n$. Accordingly a^j and b^j overlap nontrivially (not merely in a less than j-adic trope). Being equivalence classes (apart from their less than j-adic members), $a^j = b^j$ for all $j \leq n$. So $a = b$ (provided that a and b are no longer than n). A drawback of Ξ^n is that it makes all individuals exist in every possible world (cf. §1E8). In the absence of Ξ^n, collimation must be assumed.

2B7 Syntropy

Like monadic tropes (§1E4), a polytrope may be uniquely determined by its universal, its individuals, and their order. Such a universal is *syntropic*. It can be instantiated in only one way by a given sequence of individuals. Not all universals are syntropic; those that are not generally become syntropic when adverbially modified (and thus subdivided). Only syntropic universals have negations (§3A3).

2B8 Plenitude

With a view to negative universals, I make a further assumption (not otherwise needed). Where $a_1, \ldots, a_n$ are individuals (bundle-chains) and R^n is an n-adic relation,

$$a_1^{1} \cap \ldots \cap a_n^{n} \cap R^n \neq \Lambda.$$

This extends *plenitude* as assumed in §1E5. Together with syntropy, it correlates with a unique trope (existent or not) each way of instantiating a syntropic universal. If we define

$$\S R^n a_1 \ldots a_n =_{df} a_1^{1} \cap \ldots \cap a_n^{n} \cap R^n,$$

then $\S R^n a_1 \ldots a_n$ will be a singleton when R^n is syntropic. In that case, I shall also write '$\S R^n a_1 \ldots a_n$' for '$\iota \S R^n a_1 \ldots a_n$', the sole member of the singleton. ('ι' is the definite descriptor, picking out the correlated unique trope.) The definiend here may be read as 'the R^n-ing of $a_1, \ldots, a_n$'.[6]

2B9   Simple relational instantiation

Simple instantiation was explicated in §1E7, following Williams, as intersection. Socrates instantiates wisdom in world w if and only if Socrates (a concurrence bundle), wisdom (a likeness bundle), and w all overlap. We are now in a position to extend that account to relational instantiation. Let us begin with a simple dyadic case. John and Mary instantiate love in w, or John bears love to Mary in w, if and only if John[1], Mary[2], love, and w all overlap:

$$j^1 \cap m^2 \cap L^2 \bigcirc w, \quad \text{i.e.,} \quad §L^2jm \bigcirc w.$$

(For the overlap symbol '$\bigcirc$', see §1D7.) Given syntropy, this becomes

$$§L^2jm \in w,$$

(with '§' for 'ι§'). More generally, where e is exemplification or instantiation,

$$\langle a_1, \ldots, a_n \rangle \text{ e } R^n{}_w \text{ iff } §R^na_1 \ldots a_n \bigcirc w.$$

Thus, just as in the monadic case, instantiation is intersection. This development goes beyond anything Williams envisaged, but it is somewhat in the spirit of his work. In any case, it is the way to provide a unified account of instantiation in trope theory.

2C   Representatives instead of Bundles

2C1   Representatives of universals

The construction of individuals as bundle-chains may well strike even the sympathetic reader as unduly baroque. Basically, it is

motivated by the fact that an individual may not be uniquely
determined by its monadic properties: its relational properties also
count. With relational properties comes the need to distinguish
argument-places or aspects: which place in the relation does the
individual occupy? The different i-bundles in the bundle chains
are designed to cater for the different argument-places. An alternative account of individuals is possible on the assumption that
the bundles identified above with universals have kernels in the
sense of note 23. For we can then choose a kernel from each such
bundle P (arbitrarily or according to some rule) as its *representative*
$\dot{P}$, and take $\dot{P}$ rather than P as the universal.

The election of the representative "universal" $\dot{P}$ is reminiscent
in some ways of the "painless universals" Campbell (1990: 50ff)
finds in Williams (1986). There is the difference that Williams and
Campbell's painless universal, though a particular trope, is not
always the same trope, but rather indifferently any serviceable
instance of P.

2C2   Representatives of individuals

The i-bundles also have kernels, namely each at least i-adic
member trope. In particular, $\S\Xi^n a \dots a^{(n)}$ is a kernel of a^i ($i \le n$).
It can accordingly serve as the representative of each bundle a^i and
hence of the bundle-chain a. This representative $\dot{a}$ may now be
"identified" with the individual.

2C3   Instantiation of representatives

We can then redefine instantiation as a relation among representatives rather than bundles. In the monadic case, Socrates will have
wisdom in world w just in case Socrates (the representative)
concurs with some w trope that is like wisdom (an arbitrarily
chosen wisdom trope). We can accordingly define monadic instan-
tiation in w as $I^1|(w|H)$ (the relative product of 1-concurrence
and likeness as left-confined to w). In other words,

$$\dot{a}e\dot{P}_w \text{ iff } \exists t \in w: \dot{a}I^1 t, tH\dot{P}.$$

The generalization to relational instantiation is straightforward:

$$\langle \dot{a}_1, \ldots, \dot{a}_n \rangle \mathrm{e} \dot{R}^n \text{ iff } \exists t \in w: \ tI^1\dot{a}_1, \ldots, tI^n\dot{a}_n, tH\dot{R}^n.$$

On this approach, then, both universals and individuals belong to our basic ontological category of tropes. Emancipated from their bundle-chains, individuals recoup their simplicity.

The appointment of representatives from equivalence classes is a common move in mathematics. Yet here it strikes me as a metaphysical contrivance. Wisdom is surely what all wisdom-tropes have in common, not just some particular trope. Socrates is what all his tropes have in common, not just his Ξ^n-ness or whatever. Accordingly, I shrink from the formally attractive step of replacing bundles and bundle-chains by single-trope surrogates.[7] Let us carve reality at the joints when we can locate them.

2C4   Real relations

Aside from the technical details, the essential purport of this chapter could be summed up thus: taking relations seriously in trope theory. Alternative approaches seem to be animated by a devaluation of relations, a deep-seated hunch that they are "the least of the things that are", as Campbell has approvingly quoted Aristotle (1990: 97ff). But it is one of the few unequivocal metaphysical lessons of modern logic that relations are indispensable to an account of the world. It's all very well to fantasize them as a "supervenient" free lunch; but save for ontological anorectics, the consequent inanition holds little charm, least of all in desert landscapes.

3

Compound Universals, Wholes, and States of Affairs

3A Compound Properties

3A1 Modes of composition

From what might be called "atomic metaphysics", we turn now to "metaphysical chemistry". Tropes can combine to form compound states of affairs, molecular facts. Individuals can become parts of complex wholes. And properties and relations, simple universals, join to make compound universals. These are most clearly illustrated by the monadic case, compound properties; the extension to relations is then a matter of course. The most fundamental modes of property composition to consider are trope-theoretic analogues of the Boolean operations of complementation, union, and intersection; namely, negation, disjunction, and conjunction. Subsective adverbial modification is also straightforward.

3A2 Localized properties

A syntropic property P is a class of like tropes, some of which may exist in world w, others of which may not. (For 'syntropic', see §1E4.) To say of a trope such as Helen's beauty that it exists in world w is just to say that it is an element of w, or intuitively that in w Helen is beautiful. The tropes in the property P that exist in w make up P_w, P as *localized* to w:

$$P\text{-in-}w = P_w = P \cap w.$$

The connection with instantiation (§146) is obvious: a has P in w, or

$$a \text{ e } P_w \text{ iff } a \bigcirc P \cap w \text{ iff } a \cap P \bigcirc w.$$

3A3   Negative properties

The tropes in P that don't exist in w make up the negation of p in w:

$$\bar{P}_w = P - w.$$

Thus each world divides each syntropic property P into two parts, a positive half and a negative half (either of which may be empty). Syntropy guarantees that a particular a will overlap at most one of these halves: it will not have both P and $\bar{P}$ in w. And plenitude (§1E5) guarantees that a will overlap at least one half, in accordance with the law of excluded middle. Together these assumptions ensure the adequacy of our definition of $\bar{P}$ in the following sense:

$$a \text{ e } \bar{P} \text{ iff } a \notin P_w,$$

i.e.,

$$a \bigcirc P - w \text{ iff } a \cap P \cap w = \Lambda$$

for syntropic properties P. (Left to right: syntropy/noncontradiction; right to left: plenitude/excluded middle.) Like P_w, $\bar{P}_w$ is a *localized* property. Syntropic properties and their negations will be called *polarized* properties.

3A4   Disjunctive properties

In his theory of universals Armstrong rules out disjunctive properties (1978b: 19–23). They can indeed seem contrived, lacking any unified basis. In trope theory, however, they look quite natural, as we have already noted (§1D9). The disjunction of two localized properties is simply their union:

$$(P \vee Q)_w = P_w \cup Q_w.$$

The adequacy of this definition is guaranteed by

$$a \text{ e } (P \vee Q)_w \text{ iff } a \text{ e } P_w \text{ or } a \text{ e } Q_w,$$

which follows from the Boolean distribution law

$$a \cap (P_w \cup Q_w) = (a \cap P_w) \cup (a \cap Q_w).$$

3A5 Complication

With that we have the rudiments of a theory of compound properties. The theory as so far developed has limitations, however. First, it applies only to properties localized to some world; this limitation is easily lifted (§3A8). More seriously, negation has to be restricted to *syntropic* properties. Otherwise, for example, we might expect double negation $\bar{\bar{P}}$ to bring us back to the property P we started with, in accordance with §3A3:

$$\bar{\bar{P}}_w = P - w - w.$$

But $P - w - w$ is the same as $P - w$, the negative rather than the positive. Thus it cannot be applied to disjunctions to express conjunction via De Morgan's law. Notwithstanding the adequacy of $-$ and $\cup$ for Boolean algebra, our $^-$ and $\vee$ do not therefore enable us to define conjunctive properties.

Nor can they be defined by intersection, as we might expect:

$$(P \text{ \& } Q)_w = P_w \cap Q_w \quad \text{[inadequate]}.$$

For there is no guarantee in general that coinstantiated properties will overlap. In §1D4 I left open the possibility that redness and orangeness might overlap in a trope that was like all their elements.

But there will often be no trope like the members of both P and Q. For example, let P be redness and Q be rectangularity. Then it is unlikely that anything could be both a redness-trope and a rectangularity-trope: $P_w \cap Q_w$ would be empty and therefore without instances. Yet the surface of a certain brick might well be both red and rectangular in a world w, and hence instantiate $(P \ \& \ Q)_w$. Thus we see the inadequacy of the above definition.

To define conjunctive properties adequately, we shall first have to complicate slightly our conceptions of particulars, properties, and possible worlds. We replace each proto-particular (§1E3) by its power set. And we replace each simple property or possible world by its *singleton set*, the set of the singletons of all its members. In view of

$$\{x\} \in 2^a \text{ iff } x \in a,$$

the results of §§1E7, 3A2–3A4 are all preserved under this more complicated conception, which now makes conjunction possible.

3A6   Conjunctive properties

The conjunction of two localized properties is the set of united pairs spanning the two:

$$(P \ \& \ Q)_w = P_w \cdot Q_w = \mathbf{U}``(P_w \times Q_w)$$
$$= \{y \cup z: y \in P_w, z \in Q_w\}.$$

$P_w \cdot Q_w$ is van Fraassen's notation for what he calls the *product* of P_w and Q_w (1975: 227). Indeed, this theory of compound properties owes a lot to van Fraassen's theory of facts. This definition will be adequate if

$$a \ \mathrm{e} \ (P \ \& \ Q)_w \text{ iff } a \ \mathrm{e} \ P_w \text{ and } a \ \mathrm{e} \ Q_w,$$

which is fairly easily proved. (Remember that the proto-particular a is now a power set, and that if $\{x, y\} \in P_w \cdot Q_w$, $\{x\}$ may be in P_w or Q_w, and $\{y\}$ vice versa.) It's curious that conjunction should turn out to be so much more complicated than disjunction, even though conjunctive properties seem more natural than disjunctive ones. A peculiar consequence of the above definition is that often

$$(P \,\&\, P)_w \neq P_w.$$

But this is all right, since in any case

$$a \in (P \,\&\, P)_w \text{ iff } a \in P_w.$$

(On this basis we might want to consider equating the properties P and $P \,\&\, P$.)

3A7 Boolean closure

We now have modes of composition of properties corresponding to the three standard Boolean operations. But negation is still restricted to simple properties; it cannot be applied to conjunctions or disjunctions. There is no need to do so, however. As is well known, every Boolean expression has an equivalent disjunctive normal form, a union of intersections of atoms or their complements. Correspondingly, every localized compound property will have a disjunctive normal form, a disjunction of conjunctions of localized polarized properties. Only simple properties need be negated. Thus our three modes of composition already enable us to form a property corresponding to any Boolean compound.[1]

3A8 Global compounds

The compound properties so far developed are localized to particular worlds. Global properties may now be defined as functions from worlds w to localized properties P_w:

$$P = \lambda w P_w,$$

where P is simple or compound. These functions look very like the intensions of intensional model theory. Unlike intensions, however, they do not take extensions as values. For example, cordateness and renateness have the same extension in the actual world α, but cordateness-in-α is not the same localized property as renateness-in-α, since cordateness tropes are not renateness tropes.[2]

3A9 Adverbs

The account of compound properties in trope theory permits an elegant treatment of monadic adverbs (and qualifying adjectives, as opposed to predicative adjectives). To simplify the development, I will ignore the elaboration of §§3A5ff to handle conjunction. It is a commonplace that 'Dion walks slowly' cannot be analyzed as 'Dion walks and Dion is slow.' All the same, it is possible to treat slowness as a property, indeed a property of Dion (his doing something or other slowly), intersecting walking, another such property. Thus the explication of instantiation as overlapping (§1E7) extends naturally to adverbial contexts:

Dion is walking slowly iff Dion ∩ walking ∩ slowness ○ w.

Neither property is syntropic (§1E4): Dion might also be chewing slowly or (in another possible world) walking fast. But the intersection of these two properties, walking slowly, is syntropic (let us say; i.e., no more specific adverbial qualification is possible.) Like other properties, slow walking will intersect different worlds in different ways. Thus Dion may have it in some worlds but not in others, even if he is walking in all of them.[3]

In this way we get the effect of predicate modification without having to posit an extra category of functions from properties to properties. In effect, intersection with slowness (or any other adverbial property) cuts out a slice of the original property (walking), a different slice (perhaps) for each world. The monadic adverbs and adjectives thus accommodated are the ones Partee (1971) has called *subsective*. It remains to be seen how to handle other kinds of adverb and qualifying adjective, such as alienant ones ("counterfeit", "former"). Polyadic adverbs will be taken up in §3B3.

Adverbial modification applies to nonsyntropic properties,

usually turning them into syntropic ones. Where the nonsyntropic properties are simple, it seems odd to call their adverbial modifications compound. They might be better called "subproperties".

3A10   Abundance of properties

It is entirely a matter of application how many simple properties there are. We might want to limit simple properties to natural properties as a basis for what David Lewis calls a *sparse* theory of properties (1986: 59). In his earlier theory of universals, Armstrong (1978b) also keeps *compound* universals sparse by ruling out negative and disjunctive universals. This kind of sparseness is not deliberately sought here (nor is it shunned). So far as compounds are concerned, this is a fairly *abundant* theory of universals. It might be argued that sparseness constraints give a theory some of its explanatory power. If so, that kind of power is disclaimed here. It's too early to guess how few simple properties we may need, or how many compounds we shall find convenient.

3B   Compound Universals

3B1   Generalization to relations

This account of compound properties is easily extended to relations. We recall from chapter 2 that polyadic universals, relations, like properties, were loose likeness bundles, similarity classes of tropes. As in §3A5 above, those tropes are now replaced by their singletons (unit classes). Similarly, each i-bundle in the bundle-chain making up an individual is replaced by its power set. (While these elaborations are for the most part taken for granted from here on, it will still occasionally be intuitively clearer to revert to the simpler conception of chapters 1 and 2, as we indeed just did in §3A9.) These changes preserve the form of relational instantiation (§2B9). What's more, they preserve the result of part 3A, with $\langle a_1^{\,1}, \ldots, a_n^{\,n} \rangle$ in place of a. Thus our theory of compound properties generalizes to a theory of compound universals of any degree. Certain new problems arise, however.

3B2   Heterogeneous compounds

Relational instantiation was defined in §2B9 only for the case where the number of terms matches the degree of the relation. What, then, are we to make of

$$\langle a, b \rangle \text{ e } (F \& L^2)_w$$

("Alice is a female lover of Bill")? By §3A6 it breaks down into the two conjuncts

$$\langle a, b \rangle \text{ e } F_w \text{ and } \langle a, b \rangle \text{ e } L^2{}_w.$$

The former has as yet been given no meaning. In analogy to §2B9, we should expect it to become

$$a^1 \cap b^2 \cap F \bigcirc w.$$

But does b^2 overlap F? Yes, trivially, by right-inflation of b^2: as a 2-bundle, it contains all monotropes, including a's F-ness (cf. §2B4). And this works generally: §2B9 may be extended to permit arbitrarily longer sequences of terms to instantiate a relation of given degree. By similar analogy, it is natural to let

$$a \text{ e } L^2{}_w \text{ iff } a^1 \cap L^2 \bigcirc w,$$

$$\text{i.e.} \quad \S L^2 a \bigcirc w:$$

Alice instantiates love iff she loves something. This is not enough to give us the effect of existential quantification generally.

3B3   Non-Boolean compounds

Our treatment of relational expressions is beginning to resemble predicate-functor logic, to which I adverted in §2B4. What about the other modes of predicate composition afforded by predicate-functor logic: quantification (including cropping or derelativization), inclusion, padding, permutation of various kinds? In effect, the orthodox model theory for predicate-functor logic (e.g. Bacon 1985) embodies a particularistic theory of universals.[4] (Particulars, or individuals, are assumed as basic and everything else is constructed out of them by set-theoretic means.) When generalized to higher orders, it gives rise to combinatory logic, which Fitch (1952: 199) has compared to the ontological theory of Plato's (1892). It would be interesting to see whether the present scheme can be extended to comprise all the predicate functors, thereby furnishing an alternative semantics for predicate-functor logic. Since predicate-functor logic is equivalent to the conventional predicate calculus, and the semantics of the latter can be formulated trope-theoretically (see Bacon 1988), it seems likely that such a predicate-functor extension is possible. It would permit the formation of such compound properties as loving a male or compound relations like "male beloved of" out of maleness and loving.

3B4 Dyadic adverbs

In addition to monadic adverbs and qualifying adjectives (§3A9), there are dyadic ones, as in

   Atalanta runs faster than Melanion.

It might at first seem that 'faster than' here is monadic, modifying 'runs'. But compare:

   Penelope weaves faster than she unravels.
   Eric dictates faster than Claire writes.

Here 'faster than' seems to join two predicates to form a dyadic predicate. We can now make the same move as with monadic adverbs: construe 'faster than' and other dyadic adverbs as applying to tropes rather than properties:

   Atalanta's running is faster than Melanion's.
   Penelope's weaving is faster than her unraveling.
   Eric's dictation is faster than Claire's writing.

The only trouble is that now we can no longer take the adverb to denote a property, a likeness bundle of tropes. Rather, a dyadic adverb will have to stand for a set of trope *pairs*, i.e. a metarelation. This is a somewhat unwelcome outcome ontologically. So far metarelations were limited to a few structuring devices – bundlers. Now we may well be obliged to admit many other metarelations corresponding to dyadic adverbs and qualifying adjectives.

This fate can be avoided by extending likeness to trope pairs, generating sets of trope pairs as the resulting similarity classes. Such a move would have the effect of making likeness heterogeneous, both dyadic (between tropes) and tetradic (relating two pairs of tropes). It seems a bit artificial. Furthermore, triadic adverbs might call for hexadic likeness, and so on. I leave it open whether it is helpful to generalize likeness in this way.

3B5 Structural properties

An important variety of non-Boolean compound is what Armstrong has called a structural property (1978b: 69ff, 80). It is a property that something has in virtue of properties and relations of its proper parts. Examples might be right-handedness and hydrogen-atomhood, perhaps also snub-nosedness.[5] Given mereological notions, it appears that structural properties can be constructed with the help of conjunction and existential quantification (Quine's cropping, in predicate-functor logic). Thus I (j) am right-handed iff

$$\exists x \exists y (Hx \ \& \ Hy \ \& \ R^2xy \ \& \ x \ \P\P \ j \ \& \ y \ \P\P \ j \ \& \ D^2xy)$$

(H: hand; R^2: to the right of in rest position; $\P\P$: proper part of; D^2: more dextrous than). The pervasiveness of structural properties in our conceptualization of the world highlights the desirability of including predicate functors as a mode of compounding universals.

3C Compound Individuals

3C1 Compound proto-particulars as wholes

The compounding of particulars might seem to be the clearest mode of composition of all, systematically formalized in mereology, the calculus of individuals, the logic of part and whole. Williams (1953: 81), as we have seen, and following him Campbell (1981: 483; 1990: 103), take particulars or individuals (our proto-particulars) to be the mereological sum of their tropes. There are two difficulties with this conception, however.

3C2 The proper-part problem

First, an analogue of the companionship problem (§1D5, ch. 1 n. 20) arises with compound proto-particulars. Take, for example, Williams's lollipop Boanerp, with its stick Merrinel (1953: 75). Since Merrinel is part of Boanerp, Merrinel's parts, its constituent tropes, are parts of Boanerp too, though not vice versa. Thus Merrinel is mereologically contained in Boanerp and the two share some tropes. This is incompatible with Boanerp and Merrinel's both being proto-particulars in the sense of trope theory: they ought to be *disjoint* bundles. Even if we relaxed concurrence to a similarity relation, one bundle could not properly contain another, as Boanerp does Merrinel (cf. 1D1 n. 20). This mereological analogue of Carnap's companionship problem is the proper-part problem.

3C3 A set-theoretic version

The problem strongly discourages us from taking proto-particulars as mereological sums. Let us go back to particular bundles as sets, as equivalence classes. Now Merrinel, we shall want to say, is a (mereological) part of Boanerp; but Merrinel's member tropes are not members of Boanerp. This way out of the proper-part problem is closed to us, however, if we adopt a rather compelling proposal of David Lewis's (1988). Lewis suggests that the subset relation just *is* the part–whole relation as applied to classes. In that case, in being a part of Boanerp, the equivalence class Merrinel is in fact a subset, so whatever is in Merrinel is also in Boanerp. Once again, the two overlap, which is impossible for equivalence classes.

The situation becomes even clearer when we take account of the elaboration of proto-particulars into their power sets (§3A5). For the mereological sum of the power set, on Lewis's proposal, is just its union, i.e. the original equivalence class. Any subset of Merrinel (any member of its power set) will then be a subset of Boanerp.

We could elude this set-theoretic variant of the proper-part problem by rejecting Lewis's proposed grounding of set theory in mereology. Such a ploy would seem desperate, however, even if Lewis's proposal, so far as I know, has yet to be put to a thorough test.

3C4 Trope leakage

Closely connected to the proper-part problem is the problem of leakage of tropes from part to whole. The stick Merrinel consists *inter alia* of tropes of slenderness, woodenness, and beigeness, let us say. Meanwhile, Boanerp is mostly round and brown, except for its handle. Now, if Merrinel is the sum of its tropes and is part of Boanerp, it appears that Boanerp will include a woodenness trope. Being thus wooden, Boanerp will not be a popular stocking-stuffer, at least in our family. Worse, Boanerp will apparently be both beige and brown. If that doesn't sound too bad, Heraplem (Boanerp's peppermint mate) will be both beige and red, both slender all through and mostly round. Williams's mereological conception of particulars thus leads to trope leakage from part to whole.

3C5 The solution

I see just two solutions to our problem. (1) Deny that one proto-particular can ever be a proper part of another. (2) Deny that tropes are parts of proto-particulars in the same sense in which particulars can be parts of one another. Solution (1) would have the effect of turning every proto-particular into an atom in the sense of §1C4, if we read 'part of' for 'basic to'. It would thus be incompatible with the fundamental trope-theoretic strategy of construing ordinary individuals as concurrence bundles. For ordinary individuals enter into all sorts of part–whole relations.

We are left with solution (2): if tropes are "parts" of proto-particulars, they are not so in the same sense in which individuals can be parts of one another. This solution is suggested by Williams' 'fine or subtle part' as against 'gross part' (1953: 77). In adopting it, I reject Lewis's intriguing explication of class inclusion, or at any rate take him to be employing a different sense of 'part' from Williams' 'gross part', which denotes the ordinary part–whole relation. It is then comparatively unimportant whether we identify Lewis's 'part' with Williams' 'fine part'.

3C6   Compound individuals as wholes

If proto-particulars are not wholes made up of tropes as "gross" parts, the same goes *a fortiori* for individuals in the full sense, bundle-chains. For even if, contrary to solution (2) above, the several *i*-bundles in a chain were trope sums, it would still not be admissible to fuse them all together into one big whole. Their order would be lost, just as if they were all united set-theoretically (which would come to the same thing on Lewis's proposal).

Although individuals as bundle-chains are not mereological sums of tropes, they can nevertheless fuse mereologically into compound individuals. The part–whole relation involved, Williams' "gross part of", receives no special trope-theoretic explication. Beyond the well-known modeling of mereology in set theory, or the converse modeling suggested by Lewis, trope theory has nothing to contribute here. The compounding of particulars is not a part of trope theory but a significant extension of it.

3D   Compound States of Affairs

3D1   Conjunction: preliminary account

Having begun by invoking some intuitions expressed in Wittgenstein (1922), it is natural for us to expect to be able to compound tropes or states of affairs in ways analogous to the usual logical modes of sentence composition.[6] The easiest mode of composition to deal with is conjunction. Following van Fraassen (1975: 225), we could take the conjunction of two tropes s and t to be the set $\{s, t\}$. The conjunction of such compounds would then be their union. Such a conjunctive "trope" or state of affairs c would obtain in a possible world w, conceived as a set of tropes, iff $c \subseteq w$. To be sure, in §3A5 we replaced possible worlds by their singleton sets. In the present context it would be more convenient to use their power sets. Then

c obtains in w iff $c \in 2^w$.

c here could even be a singleton $\{t\}$ (cf. van Fraassen 1975: 226). It is then a mere terminological question whether we want to call $\{t\}$ a simple or a compound state of affairs. It seems more natural to call it simple, in which case we have a contrast between the trope t and the simple state of affairs $\{t\}$. I shall not adopt this terminology, however, for this approach to conjunction does not generalize to disjunction and negation (although it could obviously handle universal quantification).

3D2 Disjunction: preliminary account

Although the above account of conjunctive states of affairs does not generalize to disjunction, it is dual to a similarly simple (though incompatible) treatment of disjunction. Take the union $\{s,t\}$ now as the *disjunction* of $\{s\}$ and $\{t\}$, and similarly for compounds. Then the dual obtainment condition for a disjunctive state of affairs d would be

d obtains in w iff $d \bigcirc w$.

But this does not generalize to conjunction and negation (although it does to existential quantification).

3D3   Disjunction and conjunction: preliminary account

Disjunction and conjunction can be combined if we replace $\{t\}$ by $\{\{t\}\}$ as the state of affairs corresponding to the trope t. Then disjunction is still union, as in §3D2. For conjunction we use van Fraassen's product (cf. §3A6) above. Now the obtainment condition for any state of affairs p is

$$p \text{ obtains in } w \text{ iff } p \bigcirc 2^w.$$

It is easily verified that

> $p \cdot q$ obtains in w iff p obtains in w and q obtains in w
> $p \cup q$ obtains in w iff p obtains in w or q obtains in w

But this account, borrowed essentially from van Fraassen (1975: 227), does not extend to negation. (Van Fraassen gets negation by presupposing "complexes" with negative relations which in the present context would become negative tropes.)

3D4   States of affairs in general

Notice that in the previous section states of affairs have become sets of sets of tropes. Now a set of tropes, we said originally, was a possible world (§1B2). Thus the states of affairs of §3D3 are sets of possible worlds in that sense. But these we now recognize as special cases of what are usually called *propositions* in modal logic, or *proto-propositions* by Cresswell in a context very similar to ours (1973: 42). I shall continue to call them states of affairs. But once this connection is recognized, it becomes clear that there could be other such states of affairs, other world sets, besides those used in §3D3. Indeed, if we let any world set be a state of affairs, they will form a power-set algebra like the algebra of propositions that arises in the model theory of modal logic. This gives us the desired Boolean operations on states of affairs.

3D5   The algebra of states of affairs

Let T be the set of all tropes (or, in conformity with §3A5, trope singletons). Its power set $W = 2^T$ is the set of all possible worlds.[7] (For particular applications, e.g. color incompatibility, we might want to use just part of W.) The power set 2^w is the set of all states of affairs. (T, W, and 2^W correspond to Cresswell's **B**, **W**, and **PP** (1973: 42).) We define the state of affairs $[v]$ corresponding to a trope set v (a possible world, actually) as the set of all worlds overlapping v:

$$[v] = \{w: v \bigcirc w \subseteq T\}.$$

Where v is a singleton $\{t\}$, $[\{t\}]$ is abbreviated as $[t]$, the "simple" state of affairs that t exists. (Cf. Lewis's proposition $O(e)$, the occurrence of event e (1973b: 562).) The construction of $[t]$ is clearly reversible: $t = \imath \bigcap [t]$: there is a one-to-one correspondence between tropes and simple states of affairs. Conjunction, disjunction, and negation are now just the Boolean operations of intersection, union, and complementation with respect to W:

$$p \,\&\, q = p \cap q$$
$$p \vee q = p \cup q$$
$$\sim p = W - p$$

A state of affairs p obtains in w iff $w \in p$. It now follows from the most elementary set-theoretic considerations that

$$w \in p \,\&\, q \text{ iff } w \in p \text{ and } w \in q$$
$$w \in p \vee q \text{ iff } w \in p \text{ or } w \in q$$
$$w \in \sim p \text{ iff } w \notin p$$

for all $w \in W$, just as we would expect. Thus we have Boolean compounds of states of affairs.

3D6   Quantificational states of affairs

Since generalized intersection and union are not limited to finite sets, they give us universal and existential quantification too. A state of affairs may be given as a function of some individuals, as e.g. the state of affairs $[\S Fa]$ is a function of a. Where the state of affairs $p(a)$ is a function of the individual a, we can define the corresponding universal quantification as

$$\forall x p(x) = \bigcap_{x} p(x),$$

where 'x' ranges over individuals. Existential quantification works out similarly as generalized union.

For the special case of quantified simple states of affairs, an interesting simplification becomes possible. Since F is a likeness bundle of all the F-nesses, F will be universal in w if $F \subseteq w$. Thus

$$\forall x[\S Fx] = \{w: F \subseteq w \subseteq T\}.$$

Similarly,

$$\exists x[\S Fx] = [F] = \{w \in W: F \bigcirc w\}.$$

3D7   Limiting cases

The attentive reader will have noticed that the set 2^W of states of affairs includes the limiting cases Λ and W, the impossible and the necessary state of affairs. Since Wittgenstein (1961) these have been viewed askance, particularly since 'state of affairs' is frequently taken to mean "possible state of affairs". Nevertheless, acceptance of these two extreme states of affairs is implicit in the formation of compounds. Given a state of affairs, $\sim$ and $\&$, we can form Λ, and similarly W. Odd or degenerate though they be, compounding commits us to acknowledge them.

3D8   An alternative approach

There is a certain redundancy in a scheme involving both compound universals and compound states of affairs. Why not just use the former to construct the latter? This is in fact feasible with the help of a very fruitful device that is generally useful for representing tropes in a substance–attribute context. Where F, G, and R are syntropic, we may represent a's being F by the pair $\langle F, a \rangle$, and a's bearing R to b as the triple $\langle R, a, b \rangle$, and so on.[8] In §5C6 (cf. Bacon 1988, 1989), I show that, given certain constraints, if we begin thus with universals and particulars, the resulting tuples exhibit the same structure that tropes do. Now, having already constructed compound universals (parts 3A–3B), we could simply put them in the initial slots of such tuples. Thus a's being F and G would become

$$\langle F \,\&\, G, a \rangle$$

rather then

$$[\S Fa] \cap [\S Ga]$$

as in §3D5. A "compound trope" like $\langle F \,\&\, G, a \rangle$ obtains in w just in case $a \in (F \,\&\, G)_w$. It is fairly easily seen that this co-implies

$$w \in [\S Fa] \,\&\, w \in [\S Ga].$$

So it doesn't really matter which construction we use in this case. The tuple approach doesn't work for a's being F and b's being G, however, in the absence of a way of forming the Cartesian product of F and G (a predicate functor; cf. §3B3). Besides being more widely applicable, the state-of-affairs approach will be handy when we get to belief.

3D9   Compounds constructed

With that we have constructed compound universals and states of affairs within trope theory with the help of elementary set-theoretic operations. Our treatment of compound universals constitutes a major part of a theory of universals. Our treatment of states of affairs forms a natural adjunct to that theory. On the other hand, the trope basis has yielded no distinctive approach to compound individuals. (Actually, conjunctive and disjunctive proto-particulars could be developed in analogy to conjunctive and disjunctive properties, but they would seem to be mere curiosities.) Individuals combine as parts to form wholes, but that is a matter for mereology, not trope theory.

4

Semantics, Modality, and
World-lines

4A Trope-semantics without Metarelations

4A1 The best metaphysical explanation

So far I have set out the trope philosophy as a metaphysic. Armstrong (1978a: 64ff, 103; 1978b: 33) and Devitt (1984: 40) criticize attempts to draw fundamental metaphysical conclusions from semantic premises. Metaphysics is indeed more basic. Yet philosophers of language in our century cannot have been totally misguided in looking to semantics for metaphysical clues. Among the things to be explained by an adequate metaphysical theory is meaning, i.e. the word–world relations studied in semantics. While we don't deduce the explanans from the explanandum, we nevertheless choose the better explanans in the light of the explanandum. Lacking a logical account of "inference to the best explanation", we rightly rely on it all the same. There are two important developments in logic for which the model theory can be formulated particularly lucidly in terms of tropes: modal logic and truth-value semantics. In this part I will first look at the relation of tropes to truth-value semantics. Then in succeeding parts I will go into the foundations of modal logic in some detail.

4A2 Truth-functional trope-models

Trope theory takes tropes, rather than individuals and universals, as basic. The linguistic analogue would be to take simple sentences, rather than names and predicates, as primitive. That is what truth-value semantics does, in a sense. Simple closed sentences are treated as unanalyzed wholes, receiving the value T or F in a given model without attention to their inner subject–predicate structure. Simple open sentences are evaluated semantically in terms of their closed substitution instances. Now, if we take each simple sentence to denote (D) a trope $t \in T$, and a trope-model to contain a distinguished set of tropes $k \subseteq T$ (existent tropes; the actual world-core, if the logic were modal), then a true simple sentence S on that model will be one that denotes an existing trope: $S \in D``k$ [i.e. $D(S, t)$ for some $t \in k$]. The sentence set $D``k$ is in effect a state-description (minus the negative part). Compound sentences can then be evaluated as usual. The characteristic function of the sentence set $D``k$ will just be truth-functional valuation in the familiar sense. Provided that n-adic simple sentences are restricted to denoting n-adic tropes, the resulting modeling will be equivalent to the nonmodal, non-quantificational part of the substance-modeling given in §4B2, with trope bundles assigned to predicates and individual symbols. For if, on a given trope-model, $D(Pa, t)$, then there will be a corresponding substance-model in which $|a| \cap |P| = t$, and vice versa; and similarly for polyadic predicates and tropes.

4A3   Extension to quantification

If we wish to extend this trope-modeling to quantified sentences, while still avoiding explicit recourse to metarelations in order to construct domains, we must interpret the quantifiers substitutionally. This approach has well-known limitations when we want to quantify over more than a countable number of individuals. Such an eventuality could only arise, of course, in the context of uncountably many tropes, but such a number is in fact on the cards. Despite this limitation of trope-models, it's interesting to see how far we can go with them.

4A4   Ontological saving?

If substitutional quantification were adequate, then it would appear that we could dispense with the two metarelations of concurrence and likeness. We'd deal directly with the particular tropes, and never bother to construct individuals or relations. While that would still leave other non-ground-level relations to account for (precedence; accessibility), it suggests the possibility of a considerable ontological saving. The need for basic meta-relations is a slight embarrassment for our trope theory; it would be nice to be able to do without them. However, even if they weren't needed for extensional semantics, they appear still to be required for the analysis of belief, causation, and laws of nature. Once metarelations are relativized to worlds, the resulting world-lines become too complex to be simulated by substitutional quantification, as we shall see.

4B Transferability and Individual-concepts

4B1 Two kinds of model

So far, trope theory has given us a pleasingly simple explication of possible worlds: they are sets of tropes, we said (§1B2). We noted, however, that Williams may have intended a slightly more com-plicated notion of possible world, which is presupposed by Armstrong's transferability (trope-swapping, §§1A7, 1E6 above). According to this idea, concurrence (though not likeness) can vary from world to world. Thus a possible world becomes a set of tropes together with a concurrence relation. (The field of such a relation, apart from aspect indices, remains the whole of T, the set of all tropes, not just the world in question. Otherwise individuals would become necessary existents.) To implement this idea, we may avail ourselves of the logical device of a *modeling* (cf. Bacon 1988). In modal contexts, a modeling is a set of models represent-ing all the comprehensive ways a language might be interpreted, including requisite reference to any possible worlds involved in each model.[1] However, for purely metaphysical purposes, such models may be detached from the language they are intended to interpret and studied for the sake of their own inherent structure. A *model-structure* is a model minus its valuation or satisfaction function. Where a set of models constitutes a modeling, the corresponding set of model-structures may conveniently also be called a "modeling". We may distinguish at least two different trope-modelings of modality, then. Modelings with trope sets as possible worlds and without transferability will be called "substance-modelings", after Wittgenstein's term 'substance' for objects considered as fixed from world to world (1922: 2.024). Modelings with contingent or external concurrence will be called "world-line modelings", since they put values of world-line functions (individual-concepts) in place of substantial individuals in worlds.

4B2 Substance model-structures

A substance-modeling is a family of substance model-structures $\langle T, H, I, W, \alpha \rangle$, where $T = \bigcup_n T_n$ is the set of all first-level tropes, the union of the respective sets T_n of n-adic tropes for $n = 1, 2, 3, \ldots$; H is a similarity relation on T (likeness); I^i is almost an equivalence relation on T (except for right-inflation: §2B4) for each $i = 1, 2, 3, \ldots$ (i-concurrence); $W \subseteq 2^T$ (or perhaps $\subseteq 2^{i''T}$), a set of (possibly empty) trope sets, is the set of possible worlds; and $\alpha \in W$ (the actual world). In terms of these notions, we can define the important derivative categories of n-adic universals $P^n = \{ \text{``} X \text{''} : X \in \vec{H} \text{``} T_n \}$ (likeness-bundles of singletons of n-adic tropes) and of proto-particulars $D^0 = \vec{I}^{1}\text{``} T$ (1-concurrence bundles of tropes; in a purely monadic context, without compounds, this would be the domain of individuals.) More generally, $D^n = 2^{\vec{I}^n \text{``} T}$ (all sets of n-concurrence-bundles of tropes). The individuals of the model-structure are then a collimated (§2B6) subrelation (set of n-tuples) $D \subseteq D^1 \times D^2 \times \ldots \times D^n$ or a collimated set of infinite sequences f with $f_n \in D^n$. The domain D is thus the same for all worlds in W: it is *absolute*, not contingent or world-relative.[2]

4B3 Their modal logic

Substance model-structures correspond to the trope and polytrope models of my 1988 essay. There I showed that they characterize the oversimple system of quantified modal logic that Kripke has called **S5★**. In **S5★**, universal instantiation, existential generalization, the Barcan principle, the substitutivity of identity, and the noncontingency of identity are all valid. At first glance, that might seem an advantage, but the price is dear. Because it makes no provision for nonrigid designators, **S5★** sheds no light on various notorious modal paradoxes, such as those Carnap grouped together under 'the antinomy of the name relation' (1947: 133ff). For the philosophical logician, **S5★** is thus not very useful; for the mathematical logician it is fairly boring.

4B4   Richer modal logics

It is possible to allow nonrigid designation over an absolute domain. This is the mediating approach of my modal system **Q5** (1975b), which is closely related to Kripke's better known *Acta philosophica fennica* system (1963) and to Thomason's **Q3** (1969: 138).[3] These systems of quantified modal logic are both architectonically interesting and philosophically illuminating. Ultimately, though, a comprehensive approach is wanted in which all these systems will be special cases. Such an approach is worked out by Bressan (1972) and in my system **Q4** (1980a), building upon Thomason's delineation of **Q2** (1969: 131). Unlike **S5★**, **Q5**, **Q3**, and **Q2**, the system **Q4** allows contingent domains.[4] And no "designators", whether names or individual variables, are stipulated to be rigid as a matter of logic alone. Their rigidity can be expressed in a particular context when applicable. But names and variables stand for world-lines (individual-concepts) in the first instance. It is this feature that makes **Q4** the most nearly adequate logic to the clarification of tricky arguments involving modality and substitutivity.

4B5   World-line model-structures

The trope-modeling corresponding to the modal system **Q4** makes the domains contingent by making concurrence a contingent or external relation between tropes. A world-line modeling is a family of world-line model-structures $\langle T, H, \mathcal{J}, K, \alpha \rangle$, where T is again the set of tropes; H is a similarity on T (likeness); $\mathcal{J}$ is a family of triadic relations I such that, for each natural number i, I^i is almost an equivalence relation (except for right-inflation) in T (i-concurrence in a world); $K \subseteq 2^{i''T}$; and $\alpha \in K \times \mathcal{J} = W$, the set of possible worlds. Thus a possible world $w \in W$ is now a pair $\langle k, I \rangle$, where $k \in K$ is a "possible world" in the old sense (a set of trope singletons). k will now be called a *world-core*, the core of world w. For each $I \in \mathcal{J}$, the domains $D^1, D^2, \ldots$ are constructed as before (§4A2). This scheme allows that $\langle k, I \rangle$ and $\langle k, I' \rangle$ might be two different possible worlds, where $I \neq I'$. When $w = \langle k, I \rangle$, it will be convenient to refer to I also as I_w, to k as k_w, and to the resulting D as D_w. We now form the universe U of all functions d on W such that $d_w \in D_w$: these are the *world-lines* of our model-structure, also called *individual-concepts*. They are suited as the senses of designators rigid or nonrigid. This way of forming U is essentially standard in **Q4**-type modal systems.

Notice that if W is ordered, then the functions $d \in U$ are sequences. But each d_w is also a sequence, a bundle-chain. Thus the world-lines d are quite like two-dimensional matrices. The one dimension is aspects (argument-places), the second is worlds.

4B6   Nonrigid instantiation

The move from nontransferable to transferable tropes, from internal or absolute concurrence to external or contingent concurrence, complicates simple instantiation. First, syntropy and plenitude must be extended in the obvious way (§§2B6–2B8). $d_w{}^i$ will now be an i-bundle under the i-concurrence relation $I_w{}^i$. The 'w' index must be retained in the definition of '§':

$$\S R^n b_w \ldots d_w =_{\mathrm{df}} b_w{}^1 \cap \ldots \cap d_w{}^n \cap R^n$$

(where $b_w, \ldots, d_w$ are n in number). Simple instantiation is then once again overlapping (for simplicity, I let $n = 2$):

$$\langle j, m \rangle \ \mathbf{e} \ \mathrm{L}^2{}_w \ \text{iff} \ \S L^2 j_w m_w \bigcirc k_w$$

$$(j_w{}^1 \cap m_w{}^2 \cap L^2 \in k_w \ \text{for syntropic } L^2).$$

$L_w{}^2$ here is no longer $L^2 \cap w$, as defined in §3A2, but $L^2 \cap k_w$. Notice that $\S L^2 j_w m_w$ is now relative to world w: $\lambda w \S L^2 j_w m_w$

is a function from worlds to tropes, a trope-concept. This is the intuitive basis of the idea of a proposition developed in chapter 7.

4B7 Straight world-lines

A world-line $d \in U$ is *straight* iff, for some number i, there is a trope common to $d_w{}^i$ for all $w \in W$:

$$d \in \$ \text{ iff } \exists i \; \exists t \in T \forall w \in W \; t \in d_w{}^i.$$

Straight world-lines are reserved as the senses of rigid designators.[5] The force of this definition is perhaps easiest to appreciate if we retreat to the monadic case once again. What it says in that case is that d is straight if all its elements (values) share a trope. The trope (or those tropes) t will in a sense characterize the referent determined by d in every possible world – except that t need not obtain, so that it doesn't become an essence of d. If we admit universal tropes, i.e. tropes of the universal relation Ξ^n as in §2B6, they can serve as the common t here. Then straight world-lines would collapse into identity functions and our world-line modeling would revert to something more like a substance-modeling. (In other words, rigid designation would be secured not by nontrivial functions d across worlds but by literal identity across worlds.) But we noted that recourse to Ξ^n may be objectionable. In any event, it should be clear that straight world-lines are *collimated* (cf. §2B6). This feature combines Bressan's requirements of modal constancy and modal separatedness (1972: 49, 66ff). The interplay of straight and crooked world-lines goes a long way toward resolving various modal puzzles, anomalies that beset C. I. Lewis's paradigm of modal logic when extended to quantification in the most obvious way.[6] For on that approach variables are in effect restricted to straight world-lines, whereas a **Q4** system can quantify over straight world-lines or world-lines in general, as appropriate.

4B8 Ultimate crooks?

A technical question concerning straight world-lines is whether every individual should be the value (with respect to every world) of some straight world-line:

$$\forall w \forall x \in D_w \exists d \in \$(x = d_w).$$

We might call an x that failed to satisfy this principle an "ultimate crook", since such an x does not go straight anywhere. I find this principle plausible (Bacon 1980a: 196f), but that's all. It would have the implausible consequence that the domains of all the worlds were of equal size. To avoid that, it would be tempting to allow straight world-lines to be partial functions. But, architectonically, that would be like admitting a second mode of nonbeing, more shadowy even than nonexistence, and hence complementarily a second mode of being. Notwithstanding Bacon 1966, I would like to avoid that if possible.

4B9   The gain: intensionality

By comparing my 1989 and 1988, it will now be fairly clear how to add a semantic valuation function to a world-line model-structure to get a world-line model based on tropes. It will, furthermore, be clear how to formulate an equivalence theorem relating world-line models of an appropriate modal language (e.g. **Q4**) to **Q4**-models as in Bacon 1989 (cf. 1988: §2). I omit the details and the proof here. The upshot is that by following Armstrong in making concurrence external, and hence tropes transferable between individuals in different worlds, we gain access to the whole **Q4** apparatus of individual-concepts, rigid versus nonrigid designation, and compound intensional predicates. Little more is required to accommodate primitive intensional predication too. (An intensional predicate is one that applies in virtue of individual concepts rather than just individuals or particulars, e.g. 'popular', 'goal', 'role-model' or, as in **Q4**, 'substance'.[7]) I take this apparatus to be needed in any case if our metaphysics is to provide an adequate basis for semantics, epistemology, and the philosophy of mind. Accordingly, I forsake the Eden of a substance-modeling for the wilderness of a worldline modeling.

4C Combinatorialism

4C1 Logical atomisms

It will have been obvious, as explicitly acknowledged (e.g. §1C4), that trope theory as here developed has much in common with so-called 'logical atomism'. The same acknowledgment is made by Armstrong in his *Combinatorial Theory of Possibility* (1989a: p. ix). Logical atomism is the doctrine that the world is made up of simple facts as its ultimate constituents. For 'facts' Armstrong prefers to say 'states of affairs', but he means the same thing (1989a: 41ff).[8] I would also be prepared to employ 'facts' in my special sense (§1A3). So far, logical atomists agree in broad outline. (I would add concurrence as a constituent of the world, as I think Armstrong would likewise be committed to do were he to embrace a trope theory. Armstrong would also add, with Wittgenstein (1922: 1.11), the second-order totality fact *"und dadurch, daß es alle Tatsachen sind"*.)

4C2 Actualism vs. Meinongism

Where logical atomists part company is when it comes to non-actual possible worlds. With Russell, Cresswell (1979: 136f), Barwise and Perry (1983: 50), and Armstrong (1989a: 54) would like to make possible worlds out of recombinations of actual elements found in our world. This position in the metaphysics of modality is called "actualism". The actualist countenances as ultimate constituents of his scheme only items that exist in the actual world. The contrary view instantiates a position that has been called by the ugle name 'noneism' (Routley 1980: 2): more familiarly, 'Meinong(ian)ism'. Noneist logic has been advertised as "free logic" (Lambert 1958–64). While its fortunes seem to be rising, Meinongism remains uncongenial to Ockhamists. However that may be, what often goes unnoticed amid the politics of ideas is that the actualists are a good deal worse off when it comes to modality.[9] Thus, under Quine's influence, it was once fashionable to eschew modality and intensions altogether as "creatures of darkness". At length the repressed returned to haunt the valiant bullet-biters. "Combinatorialism"[10] has proved an insufficiently potent means of exorcism: aliens threaten.

4C3   Alien individuals

Armstrong is prepared to avail himself of alien individuals but not alien universals. 'Alien' means 'not existing in the actual world'. Have we just caught Armstrong with his hand in the Meinongian cookie jar? At first glance, it would appear not. For he grants aliens *conceptual* status:[11]

> So we can form a *fully determinate* concept of an indefinite number of alien individuals 'by analogy' . . . our alien individuals are reached . . . conceptually, 'by analogy'. (1989a: 60)

In his pegboard picture, Armstrong represents actual individuals by identical hooks:

> There are also available an indefinite further number of these hooks. These further hooks . . . represent merely possible individuals, individuals additional to the actual individuals. But all hooks are *conceptually interchangeable*. Merely to swap two hooks around . . . represents no ontological difference. (1989a: 65)

Thus Armstrong's aliens are conceptual, unlike actual objects; at the same time, they are conceptually on an ontological par with the actuals. Separate but equal, one is tempted to say. But Armstrong can't have it both ways. His combinatorial theory requires complete interchangeability. The imagined merely "conceptual" status of the aliens is not enough. They aren't available "by analogy" as mere conceptual constructs: they must be embraced as completely interchangeable with actuals. Now, items *just* like actual ones that don't exist are the stock in trade of the Meinongian. Consistency would oblige Armstrong to relinquish actualism for Meinongism.[12]

4C4   Alien tropes

But if forced into Meinongism anyhow, why fixate on alien *individuals*? For us tropes, not particular individuals, are basic. An individual not existing in the actual world, and hence disjoint from it, will contain alien *tropes*. It is with them that our Meinongism should rightly begin. An alien trope is one that either doesn't *i-concur* with any actual trope (for any *i*) or isn't like any actual trope. In other words, it could not be mimicked by recombination of elements abstractable from the actual world. Alien tropes are what I have been assuming all along (since §B2). With their help, we get a straightforward combinatorial theory of modality.

4D   Existence, Persistence, and Modalities

4D1   Individual existence

In systems of quantified modal logic like those discussed in part 4A, the existence of an individual is often equated with membership in the domain of the world in question. The classic example is Kripke's *Acta Philosophica Fennica* system. Following Thomason, however, I have made singular existence a non-universal property (§1E8). It's now time to extend that analysis from proto-particulars to individuals in the full sense (bundle-chains). On the latter conception, an individual is still made up of a bunch of tropes, but they are strung out in several bundles like beads on a string. The different beads (bundles) represent different aspects or argument-places for the individual to slot into. When does such an individual exist? Again, when one of its tropes exists (is) in the world in question:

$$E_w a \text{ iff } \bigcup_i a^i_w \bigcirc k_w.$$

This still gives us

$$E_w a \text{ iff } (\exists \varphi) \varphi a \text{ in } w$$

in the spirit of Leonard (cf. §1E8).

4D2   Persistence

An individual as determined by a straight world-line in w, if it also exists in w, is what Thomason calls a "*substance*" (1969: 137ff).

The term is apt enough. But since I have already used it in connection with so-called substance-modelings (§4A2: a closely related usage, actually), I will call existents as determined by straight world-lines (transworld) *persistents*. (Think of the worlds as analogous to times.)

$$\text{Persists}_w a \text{ iff } E_w a \ \& \ a \in \$.$$

Despite the fact that we encounter the world as a world of facts, persistents are basic to the substance–accident way we conceive of it. It could perhaps be argued that much of the travail of Western philosophy, particularly English-speaking, is traceable to a reluctance to recognize that persistents are but one special kind of world-line. The obsession with persistence (substance) is a core intuition of "empiricism". (Berkeley is no exception: he rejected matter, not persistence. Hume, having despaired of persistence, embraced skepticism.) A modern instance of this obsession is the so-called problem of sense-data (cf. Bacon 1979).

4D3   Universal accessibility: S5

Logical necessity is truth in all possible worlds of every world-line model. Metaphysical necessity is truth in all possible worlds of the intended world-line model(s) of our considered metaphysical theory. (If the theory is not yet established as true, then neither are the would-be metaphysical necessities.) Logical and metaphysical necessity have the structure of the modal system S5: they are unconditional necessities. As David Lewis has pointed out, many other modal concepts can be viewed as conditional necessities (1973a: 4ff). The condition involves in each case an accessibility relation, the heart of the modal concept in question. No such relation is needed to characterize logical and metaphysical necessity.

4D4   Reflexive accessibility: M

But not all necessity is metaphysical necessity. There is, for example, physical necessity, the necessity of physical laws. I have argued elsewhere that it is characterized by an accessibility relation that, while reflexive, is neither symmetric nor transitive (Bacon 1980b). Thus physical necessity has the structure of the modal system **T** or **M**. (Cf. Lewis 1973a: 5.) This physical accessibility relation is basic: purported definitions (e.g. in terms of 'law') are one and all circular.

4D5 *Transitive accessibility:* **S4**

Lewis has shown that in place of an accessibility relation on worlds, we can equally well use his counterpart relation on world-bound particulars (1979). Counterpart relations are closely connected with world-lines, straightness corresponding to an extreme constraint on the counterpart relation (that it be an equivalence). In the present context, one natural accessibility relation that suggests itself is this: w is accessible from u iff all persistents of w exist in u:

$$uRw \text{ iff } \forall d \in \$(E_w d_w \rightarrow E_u d_u).$$

'uRw' says that whatever persistents are found in w were already available in u. You could get w out of u without creating anything new. Clearly R is reflexive and transitive but not symmetric. Hence it characterizes the modal system **S4**. (The same would be true if we took the converse of R, which is also of interest.) In a quantificational context, this type of necessity obeys Barcan's principle:

$$\forall x \boxed{4} Fx \rightarrow \boxed{4} \forall x Fx$$

or

$$\diamondsuit \exists x Fx \rightarrow \exists x \diamondsuit Fx$$

(where 'x' ranges over persistents; the little '4' indicates **S4**-type modality). It says that there's nothing new under the sun of an accessible world. If we used the converse of R as our accessibility relation, then it would validate the converse of Barcan's principle (which is often felt to be less controversial), a kind of law of the conservation of persistents.

Our characterization of ⊡ is clear enough. Does it have a name? I suggest tentatively 'cosmological necessity', with the following considerations in mind. It is sometimes suggested that the physical laws would have been different if the universe had developed differently in the first few instants (e.g. Weinberg 1977: 26, 120f.). That conditional has a necessity stronger than *physical* necessity yet weaker than *logical* (or even metaphysical) necessity. It seems to lie somewhere in between, as does ⊡.

4D6   Modal pluralism

It is usual to pose **M**, **S4**, and **S5** as alternative formalizations of alethic modality and then to invite students to ponder which is more plausible (cf. Loux 1979: 16–24). The model-theoretic characterizations made available by Carnap, Kanger, Kripke, Hintikka, and others are supposed to aid such deliberations, but they tend to remain inconclusive. We have now seen that there is a distinctive place for each of the three kinds of modality in trope theory. We need not choose among them; each has its use. We can be modal pluralists.[13]

4D7   Modal states of affairs

In the last chapter we saw how to compound states of affairs Booleanly and quantificationally. Now we can add modal compounds. Recall that a state of affairs is a set of worlds. I shall write '$\mathscr{A}$' for '$\overleftarrow{R}$ (R as in §4D5): $\mathscr{A}(w)$ is w's accessibility sphere, the set of worlds accessible from w (cf. Lewis 1973a and Bacon 1975a). The state of affairs that (cosmologically) necessarily p, where p is itself a state of affairs, is given by

$$\boxdot p = \{w\colon \mathscr{A}(w) \subseteq p\}.$$

Dually,

$$\Diamond p = \{w\colon \mathscr{A}(w) \bigcirc p\}.$$

For logical and metaphysical modality, $\mathscr{A}(w)$ becomes W, yielding the slightly simpler definitions

$$\Box p = \{w: p = W\}$$
$$\Diamond p = \{w: p \neq \Lambda\}.$$

4D8   Other modalities

We have seen how trope theory can accommodate three versions of the most viable quantified alethic modal logics so far developed. What about other modalities? There is good reason to think that deontic logic might be reducible to alethic modal logic (Anderson 1958, 1966). More promising still, it can be based on a relation of "better-than" between tropes, as in part 9A below. Agent possibility (capacity, 'can' in the sense of 'can do') can probably be analyzed with the help of physical possibility, time, and perhaps causation.[14] But the Waterloo of modal theory has hitherto been the propositional attitudes, foremost among them *belief*. The modal apparatus developed in this chapter is no exception. Unlike ⊡, ◇, etc., Jo's-belief-that does not map states of affairs into states of affairs, any more than truth-values into truth-values. But appropriate objects of belief are not far to seek.

5

Metarelations and Metaphysics

5A Categories and the Trope Cascade

5A1 Economy of relations?

Unlike some, I have not put trope theory forward as any kind of nominalism.[1] All the same, one of its chief attractions is the promise of relative ontological economy. I wouldn't go so far as to advertise it, with Campbell (1990: ch. 1), as a one-category ontology. As we have seen, it requires at the very least a category of tropes and a category of relations of tropes, or metarelations, as I have called them. But the hope is that the tropes and their metarelations form a significantly simpler scheme than individuals together with their multifarious relations. If not, why relinquish the traditional substance–attribute approach or its particularist cousin? Well, to begin with, it may be argued that the meta-relations do indeed constitute a simpler or more homogeneous system than ordinary relations. So far we have worked with likeness and i-concurrence, the latter relativized to possible worlds (as the former will be too, §7A7). If we treat i and the worlds as terms of the metarelations, then they are two: dyadic or triadic, and tetradic, respectively. Considered as dyadic relations of tropes, on the other hand, they are legion, quite likely infinite in number, although of two types, likeness relations and concurrence relations:

$H_\alpha, H_u, H_w, \ldots \qquad I^1{}_\alpha, I^1{}_u, I^1{}_w, \ldots, I^2{}_\alpha, I^2{}_u, I^2{}_w, \ldots,$

Ordinary relations fall into no such neat pattern.

5A2   The trope structure

The set of first-level tropes T together with the metarelations R just "listed" (considered as dyadic) make up what I have called elsewhere a *trope structure* $\langle T, R \rangle$ (1989: 145). Each of these metarelations is a similarity relation between first-level tropes. In regard to such relations, Williams advocated

> an assimilation of the very categories of our theory – concurrence, similarity, abstractness, and so forth – to the theory itself, as tropes like the rest, instead of relegating them to the anomalous immunities of "transcendentals". (1953: 84)

Accordingly, the instances or cases of concurrence and likeness (first-level relations) will be second-level tropes or hypertropes. These in turn stand in second-level relations of concurrence and likeness. (Because all the first-level relations are symmetric, there is no need to distinguish second-level 1-concurrence from 2-concurrence. On levels, see ch. 1 n. 13.)

5A3   The trope cascade

I have shown (1989) how to generate a trope structure out of a simpler structure called a *trope cascade*. The instances of the second-level relations posited above would be third-level tropes ("hyperhypertropes"). If we now took *third-level tropes* as basic, we could descend again to first-level tropes as follows. Assume one third-level relation between third-level tropes, concurrence. It partitions third-level tropes into bundles, the second-level tropes (hypertropes). Also, we split the third-level tropes into two disjoint subclasses, which will serve as the second-level relations of concurrence and likeness. As applied to hypertropes (by intersection, i.e. instantiation), these yield bundles corresponding to our original first-level tropes and metarelations. But the trope cascade is a much simpler structure than the trope structure with which we began, with its plethora of metarelations. Just a set of third-level tropes, a concurrence relation, and a bifurcation of the tropes into two groups – that's all there is to a trope cascade.

Unfortunately, it looks as though the relations generated by a trope cascade are by no means the only ones we need. Before we consider accepting it as ontologically basic, we must take account of other fundamental relations.

5A4   Before and after

Some tropes come wholly before others in time. This relation can in fact be made the basis of time (§6A5 below). As a relation between tropes, a first-level relation, precedence expands the "list" of metarelations (§5A1) to be delivered by a trope cascade. The trouble is that it's not a similarity relation and it's not symmetric. It can, to be sure, be incorporated into a trope cascade if we start one level farther up, at level 4. That works, but somehow it doesn't inspire metaphysical confidence, any more than the doctrine that the elephant supporting the world is itself supported by a tortoise (Locke 1689: Book II, §XIII, p. 19).

5A5   Causation

A further important relation among tropes is causation. According to Williams, "Causation is often said to relate events, and generally speaking any event is a trope" (1953: 90). In Campbell's view, "The terms of the *causal* relation are always tropes" (1990: 22). At the same time, he recognizes that the terms may also be what he calls "events", i.e. sequences of tropes at a place (1990: 113, 122; 1981: 480; 1990: 22). Events in the latter sense are thus compounded out of tropes: they would seem to be a special kind of state of affairs. As tropes themselves correspond to simple states of affairs, a unified account can take causation as a relation between states of affairs. That is in effect what David Lewis does (calling world sets "propositions", the more usual name) in his impressive and thought-provoking analysis of causation. Lewis's first, more traditionally Humean analysis (which he doesn't endorse) makes use of logical implication by a set of natural laws (1973b: 556). For reasons given in (1980: 8f), I would replace that by physically strict implication, physically necessary → (cf. §4C4). Lewis's second analysis is based on his counterfactual implication (1973b: 5B3). Thus, if some such analysis as Lewis's has hope of success, it appears that we need not recognize causation as a basic, irreducible relation of tropes or states of affairs. Rather, we are thrown back upon some sort of implication relation. (We recall that Kant transcendentally deduced his category of causality from the hypothetical form of judgment (1787: 95, 106).)

5A6 Accessibility relations

Indeed, it seems intuitively plausible that there must be some fundamental sort of conditional or implicative relation between states of affairs and hence also between tropes. What springs immediately to mind is the strict implication ‖– defined in §7B5 as class-inclusion between states of affairs. For if it suffices, then implication, like causation, is a derivative relation, not a basic one. I fear, though, that causation and other applications call for a more complex conditionality relation than strict or logical implication: perhaps physically strict implication (Burks' causal implication (1951)); perhaps Lewis's counterfactual conditional; perhaps Anderson and Belnap's relevant conditional (1975: §28; ultimately due to Church (1951)); or perhaps a combination of all three. The first and third of these are based on accessibility relations that don't appear to be further analyzable. Lewis's conditional is based on his apparatus of nested accessibility spheres (1973a: 13f) or, equivalently, an accessibility relation together with a triadic relation of comparative similarity of worlds (1973a: 48f). In all three cases, basic relations among worlds are presupposed. The same is true of the doxastic accessibility relation on which belief is based (§7C4), and presumably analogous relations for other propositional attitudes.

5A7 Intentionality

Propositional attitudes are only the tip of the iceberg. It is characteristic of beings with minds that they can think about all sorts of things: not just individuals, not just tropes, not just universals, but equally well possible worlds, numbers, set-theoretic structures, social causes, and gods. Thus we all of us have innumerable relations with non-individuals.[2] It's fashionable nowadays in English-speaking philosophy to suppose either that such "relations" are not really relations at all, or that they supervene on the physical characteristics of thinkers, of persons, and their environment. To which I reply "Show me." Once the reduction or the supervenience has been spelt out, then we can see whether the "physical" characteristics employed are properties and relations of individuals. If so, then perhaps we are excused from assuming intentional relations and psychological accessibility relations as basic. I tend to suspect that the project is doomed, however. It's not that matter couldn't conceivably do what minds do. Rather, relations among possible worlds, including doxastic accessibility, are not in general reducible to relations of tropes, let alone relations of individuals.

5A8   Limited cascades?

A full account of the world, then, apparently requires many other relations besides relations of individuals, which reduce to trope bundles, and metarelations, which reduce to hypertrope bundles. Even if our wildest materialistic dreams came true, there'd still be the accessibility relation involved in conditionality to deal with, and probably others besides. I see no way of extending or modifying a trope cascade so as to generate these other relations. It's an intriguing device all the same. If it makes sense to replace individuals and their properties and relations by first-level tropes and their relations (the basic trope-theoretic move), why not more of the same medicine? At the third level a significant simplification is reached. Indeed, we could use the trope cascade alongside the various other relations we need, although that seems like lopsided economy.

These difficulties aside, I'm still reluctant, all things considered, to take the constructibility of a three-level trope cascade as manifesting how things are. It has the flavor of a trick, like those tiny Japanese wafers which, when placed on water, unfold into artificial flowers. The particular cascade adopted must be the one that implicitly contains just the whole trope structure we want to get out of it. What is significant about the cascade, like the Japanese wafer, is what's packed into it. Thus the trope cascade, even if possible, is hard to take seriously as an ontological reduction. This situation is mirrored epistemically: our basic experience is of first-level tropes (§§1A1, 1A3); third- or fourth-level tropes are *outré* by comparison. As a plausible compromise, then, I suggest that we content ourselves with either a slightly truncated two-level cascade $\langle T^2, R^2 \rangle$ (T^2 being the set of hypertropes) or with a trope structure $\langle T, R \rangle$ (R comprising more metarelations than we might have liked). The first alternative constitutes a fair ontological saving, since R^2 consists of just three second-level relations: 1-concurrence, 2-concurrence, and likeness. The second alternative is less parsimonious but perhaps more down to earth.

5A9   Counting categories

That leaves us with ontological atoms of at least two kinds: tropes and relations (whether first-level or second-level). Among the relations are not just trope relations but accessibility relations among possible worlds (and of possible worlds to individuals in the case of psychological accessibility[3]). Are there more? As Campbell has pointed out, tropes are immediate objects of evaluation (1981: 481). The evaluative properties employed (goodness, beauty, etc.), as first-level properties, can be abstracted from hypertropes in a second-level trope cascade. The accessibility relations needed to characterize deontic concepts, such as "ought", like other accessibility relations, relate possible worlds. Finally, as announced in part 1C, all along I've been helping myself to fundamental logical, set-theoretic, and mathematical devices. Unlike Armstrong (1989a: 134–7) and Campbell (1990: 88f),[4] I don't claim to be able to provide a metaphysical basis for set theory. Unlike Armstrong (1989a: 124–33) and Campbell (1990: 93f), I don't offer a metaphysical foundation for metaphysics either. In my view, metaphysics presupposes its basic concepts and operations. Here we have a third category of atoms (at least), a "third realm", so to speak, although logically it precedes the first. It would be hasty to declare it the last.

5A10 *Economy eked out*

As remarked at the beginning of this chapter, a main attraction of the trope philosophy is its promise of ontological economy. I have rejected the three-level trope cascade as a specious saving. Now I have affirmed a need for at least three categories of atoms, quite likely more. What has become of the economy promise?

In general, there is no royal road to categorial economy. The world is a complicated place. The point is aptly put in an anecdote by J. Harry Cotton (my first philosophy teacher):

> I recall a fellow student who was going through a healthy period of complete skepticism. At the same time he was very much in love with the girl whom he later married. "But," he confided, "I won't let any of my logical categories touch her!" So much the worse for his logical categories as this man has long since learned. (1951: 103)

That's what I feel like saying to category-choppers – so much the worse for the categories – unless they can deliver.

As Church says in another connection,

> To those who find forbidding the array of abstract entities and principles concerning them which is here propposed, I would say that the problems which give rise to the proposal are difficult and a simpler theory is not known to be possible. (1978: 171)

Yes, we need basic relations, but fewer kinds than the substance–attribute theorist of universals, it would seem. But all this deserves further investigation. In my view trope theory's most serious rival is non-nominalistic particularism, which constructs everything out of individuals by set-theoretic means. I have preferred to start with tropes because they are first for us in experience. That they are also basic to being generally is a theoretical hypothesis to be recommended for its potential fecundity.

5B   The Reality of Relations

5B1   Beyond the facts

I began by intoning "The world is everything that is the case . . . the totality of facts," the set of those tropes that exist. Later I added concurrence (§§4A1, 4A5) to the characterization of a world, retaining the set of tropes existing there as its core. It's clear that the (meta)metarelations, likeness and concurrence, as well as temporal precedence, are underdetermined by the world-core (§4A5), the first-level facts or tropes of the world. That is, given the first-level tropes in a world, no particular metarelations are set. The same goes for second-level relations as well as for the basic accessibility relations and the relations they support, such as physical necessity, causation, and belief. The question arises whether these relations are real or ideal. Do we group tropes the way we do on some objective basis, or do we contribute the grouping? Are likeness and concurrence found or imputed? There are three interesting possible answers: realism, conventionalism, and transcendental idealism. I choose realism, but the other two positions merit some consideration.

5B2   Conventionalism

On this view, the way we group tropes into individuals and universals is determined not by the way things are but by social conventions. This could cut two ways, however. The social conventions might be considered something over and above the existing tropes of the world, or they might supervene upon, be determined by, or even belong to those tropes. If the conventions have their own autonomous existence, so, presumably, do the metarelations they determine. If the conventions boil down to facts, again, so do the metarelations. For reasons given in chapter 4 and §5B1, I take the latter alternative to be ruled out. The former alternative is not so different from realism in a way, except for the mediation of society, a contingent arrangement.

5B3   Conventional likeness?

But let's look as some specific instances. Take the blueness of this pencil and its thinness – two tropes not considered alike in our society. Might some New Guinea tribe, say, allocate them to the same universal? Anything is possible, I suppose, but what would the tribe do with a yellow pencil's tropes? It all begins to sound fantastic.

5B4   Conventional concurrence?

Again, take the blueness of my pencil and the yellowness of yours. Might they 1-concur in some society? Not even convention is powerful enough to make one thing both blue and yellow in the same respect. At best, however, what these examples tend to show is that concurrence and likeness are not always a matter of convention, not that they never are. That's already enough to refute global conventionalism, but it leaves the door open to local or restricted conventionalism.

For example, a reincarnationist might find that my insouciance concurs with the relaxed attitude of a previous avatar. Is there a second-level fact of the matter, a metarelational truth, that he's wrong about? It's hard to say 'yes' with confidence. If I do, it's not that the reincarnationist has individuated incoherently, as in the case of the yellow blue pencil, but that his way of bundling individuals fits other causal patterns less well.

5B5   Transcendental idealism

This is the view that the (meta)metarelations and some of the accessibility relations are like Kant's categories: neither part of the nonmental world nor contingent projections of the way we happen to think, but necessary preconditions of our knowledge of that world. The metarelation of concurrence, which gives us objects, is reminiscent of Kant's category of substance. The accessibility relation underlying conditionality and causation brings to mind Kant's category of causality. The accessibility relation of physical modality corresponds to Kant's categories of necessity and possibility. The parallel is not exact, for our world of facts includes aspects of both Kant's noumenal and his phenomenal world. Our tropes are not featureless, unknowable things in themselves, but instances of properties and relations, many of them perceivable.

Great as we must acknowledge Kant's achievement to have been, I think that in the end we must reject the transcendental ideality of his, or our, categories as an untenable dodge. If the categories are a necessary precondition for rational knowledge, that means that in order to be rational, you must think in accordance with the categories. This seems to give the categories, or their synthetic a priori principles, a status like the laws of logic. On the other hand, if the categories are not logical laws but necessary preconditions of experience, that seems to mean that they are entailed by experience, making them very high-level empirical laws. Either way, the apriority of the categories seems incompatible with Kant's contention that in some sense they are contributed by us. If every rational thinker[5] *must* employ the categories – not just because of the way his brain happens to be wired – then there is a real ground for that *must*.

5B6   Generic categories?

Perhaps it is inappropriate to compare the (meta)metarelations and accessibility relations with Kant's categories. The latter are *formal*, although Kant manages to find some surprisingly specific content for them, e.g. Newton's laws. I take it, though, that the form of our understanding does not constrain us to think in accordance with Newton's laws specifically; it constrains us to think causally, in terms of substance, etc. The analogy for trope theory would be that we must employ some concurrence relation or other, some accessibility relation or other defining causation, and similarly for the other basic relations. Thus generic concurrence and likeness, generic accessibility of the appropriate sort, but no specifications thereof, play the role of Kantian categories.

While I think that's right, it's a platitude. (A tropophobe would, of course, put it differently. But he too would have to settle upon a domain of particulars or relations, a causal relation, etc.) Sure, we must group tropes one way or another in order to get on. But the question of this part concerned not the generic but the specific groupings employed. Do they have any objective basis? And I answer 'yes', although of course we can be wrong about it.

5B7   Realism

That two tropes r and s i-concur is an objective fact (a second-level rather than a first-level fact). That r is like s is too. ('Objective' is used here in the no-kidding sense, not in Kant's sense of 'inter-subjective' or the watered-down sense of some contemporary moral antirealists.) It may be different in other possible worlds; neither i-concurrence (nor likeness: §7A7 below) is internal. But once the actual world is singled out, it's settled not only which first-level tropes exist, but also which hypertropes (concurrings, likenesses) exist.

What about the basic accessibility relations? As I have set things up, these are not part of the actual world *per se* but of a model-structure containing a whole set of possible worlds. The same would be true of temporal precedence. A full account of reality would not just single out the actual world but an entire intended doxastic (or richer) model-structure, including accessibility relations on worlds and a precedence relation of tropes. Again, I take it to be an objective question which model-structure should be the "intended" one (to speak *sub specie aeternitatis*, as it were, as though, like Leibniz's creator God, we had the complete smorgasbord of models before us. Given our epistemic limitations, perhaps at best a certain set of model-structures would be indicated.)

Thus I hold the metarelations and the basic accessibility relations to be real in a twofold sense, in their existence and in their application. Whether or not they relate some tropes or possible worlds is a question of objective truth, independent of how you or I or any society may happen to think about it. And since for a relation to exist is to be instantiated (cf. §§1E8, 2A3), that is likewise an objective matter. To the extent that these relations have proved necessary for a metaphysical account of the world, they are instantiated and they do exist. (The tropophobe would not quite agree, of course, but cf. §5B6, end.)

5B8 Discerning the metarelations

It is all very well to posit metarelations as real, marking out individuals and universals. But to shift now from ontology to epistemology, how do we discover second-level facts of concurrence and likeness? Given two tropes, how do we know that they concur or are alike? The preliminary heuristic explanations of §§1D1, 1E2 are no real help, for they take examples for granted in which individuals and properties are already salient. Yet we must beware of expecting too much here. The problem is analogous to how we individuate objects on a more traditional substance–accident approach, problems pondered in detail by Quine (1960: 90–100), among others. When we're very little, how do we know that it's mother again (substance–accident view); i.e., how do we know that this smile (as we awake) 1-concurs with that kiss (as we dropped off)? When we're bigger, how do we determine that it's plagiarism again; i.e., how do we establish that this student's cribbing of Ayer in an essay is "like" that colleague's pinching ideas from a thesis she was supervising? In some cases we can begin to tell a story about perception and memory. In others we wheel in scientific methodology. It's no drawback of the metarelations that we can't give general epistemic criteria for their application, any more than it's a defect of the traditional substance–accident approach that it can't give general epistemic criteria for picking out objects. Either way, we seek ultimately to delineate an intended model-structure, including either a domain of individuals or metarelations H and I^i. It's not easy.

5B9 Playoff of relations

It's one thing to intend the right model-structure. It's another, for us mortals, to find it. At the more intellectual level, we, particularly the scientists among us, would naturally play one accessibility relation or metarelation off against the others. In this process, some relations may sometimes take epistemic priority over others.

For example, (tropist) empiricists would probably tend to assume that we match up some properties first, then bundle together some particulars, and finally discover some causal relations. But it might work the other way around. An incipient grasp of causes might prompt us to individuate properties and particulars in a specific way.

5B10   An example

An excessively simple example may help to make this clear. Suppose that there are just four first-level, monadic tropes in the world, A, B, C, and D, related as follows:

> A causes B
> C causes D.

Now, we might take A to 1-concur with B, and C with D, giving rise to the two (proto-)particulars $\{A, B\}$ and $\{C, D\}$, or ab and cd for short. Furthermore, we might liken A to D, and B to C, yielding the properties $\{A, D\}$ and $\{B, C\}$, for short AD and BC. The four facts obtaining in our little world can accordingly now be expressed as

> ab is AD ab is BC
> cd is BC cd is AD.

And the following two causal relations will obtain:

> $AD(ab)$ causes $BC(ab)$
> $BC(cd)$ causes $AD(cd)$.

In the one case ADness causes BCness; in the other, vice versa. No useful causal generalization is possible. But now let us change the example just to this extent: we liken A to C and B to D. Now we shall get

> $AC(ab)$ causes $BD(ab)$
> $AC(cd)$ causes $BD(cd)$,

supporting the causal generalization

$$\forall x[AC(x) \text{ causes } BD(x)].$$

Thus, while the facts and their causal interrelations do not in general determine concurrence and likeness, they constrain them, and vice versa. Epistemically, the basic relations are all in it together, grist for the mill of total science. But science and everyday poking about, when successful, discover the relations, they don't make them.

5C Five Ways to Carve Reality

5C1 Alternatives to trope theory

Trope theory is not the only basic form of metaphysic. Leaving aside for a moment complications introduced by ground-level relations, accessibility relations, evaluative properties, and world-line model-structures (world-relative concurrence, §§4B5 ff), we can distinguish five ontological approaches to metaphysics:

1 Particularism: individuals, possible worlds basic; universals constructed
2 Universalism: universals, similarities (possible worlds) basic; individuals constructed
3 Substance–attribute view: individuals, universals basic; states of affairs, possible worlds constructed
4 Trope theory: tropes, metarelations basic; individuals, universals, possible worlds constructed
5 Substance–trope theory: individuals, tropes, likeness basic; universals, possible worlds constructed.

(By 'constructed' I mean 'taken as complex structures', not 'manufactured' or 'socially constructed'.) With some oversimplification, these five basic ontological approaches can be seen as five precedence rankings of the categories exhibited in table 5.1.

Table 5.1 World-table

⋮	⋮	⋮	⋮	⋮	⋮	⋮
G	Tom's Gness	Dick's Gness	Sue's Gness	a's Gness	b's Gness	....
F	Tom's Fness	Dick's Fness	Sue's Fness	a's Fness	b's Fness	....
wisdom	Tom's wisdom	Dick's wisdom	Sue's wisdom	a's wisdom	b's wisdom	....
blondness	Tom's blondness	Dick's blondness	Sue's blondness	a's blondness	b's blondness	....
tallness	Tom's tallness	Dick's tallness	Sue's tallness	a's tallness	b's tallness	....
	Tom	Dick	Sue	a	b	....

Particularism (1) takes the individuals along the x-axis as basic. Universalism (2) takes the universals along the y-axis as basic. The substance–attribute view (3) takes both as basic. Trope theory (4) takes neither individuals nor universals as basic, but rather the tropes occupying the cells. In addition, the arrangement of the cells into rows (universals) and columns (individuals) represents the two basic metarelations of likeness (H, horizontal similarity) and concurrence (I, vertical similarity). Finally, the substance–trope theory (5) favored by Martin and Armstrong takes the individuals along the x-axis, the tropes in the cells, and their line-up as basic.

5C2 Ontological economy?

This world-table sheds some light on what is at stake in our choice of ontology. To begin with, it is no simple matter to pick out the most economical scheme. Each is a two-category ontology as far as it goes, except for substance–trope theory, which has three basic categories, and universalism, which could be construed as having one category. Particularism and universalism both assume possible worlds in some form, probably the most numerous category. The two trope theories assume tropes, the next most numerous. For low categorial cardinality, the substance–attribute view wins, all the more if it incorporates a sparse theory of universals like Armstrong's. However, in ontology the premium is pre-eminently on minimizing the number rather than the size of categories (number of elements). Thus the criterion of economy is inconclusive as a basis for preferring one or other of our five ontologies.

5C3   Equivalence of the five approaches

In my 1988 I showed that modelings of a simple quantified modal logic based essentially on the first four ontological approaches reviewed here are all in a sense equivalent. Given any modeling of one type, it is possible to construct a modeling of each of the other three types such that the same sentences are verified, the same arguments validated. A similar construction can be given here, though only with rough and approximate results, since the five ontologies involve divergences of detail and are not so strictly defined. Subject to these qualifications, an equivalence among our five ontologies, a reciprocal embeddability, can be established.

For each given type of ontology, relax the requirement that its basic items be atoms (primitive): allow the items in the basis to be constructed (defined). Call the result a *structure* of the corresponding type. For example, a particularist structure would be like a particularist ontology, except that the "individuals" and "possible worlds" in its basis might be complex. I will first show how to make a universalist structure out of a particularist ontology (or structure), then a substance–attribute structure out of a universalist one, and so on. At each stage, structure is (roughly) preserved, but no reduction is claimed.

5C4   Particularism to universalism

We begin, then, with a particularist structure $\mathcal{P}$. Its constructed properties and relations (functions from possible worlds to classes of n-tuples of individuals, invented by Kanger (1957: 2 f) and

Kripke (1959: 2)), become the "universals"[6] in the basis of a universalist structure $\mathcal{U}$. For each particularist possible world w, let two such universals be w-similar iff they are jointly instantiated in w. These w-similarities are the similarities or possible worlds in the basis of $\mathcal{U}$, which is therewith finished.

5C5   Universalism to substance–attribute

Next, take a universalist structure $\mathcal{U}$: its universals can serve as the attributes in the basis of a substance–attribute structure $\mathcal{SA}$. And the constructed individuals of $\mathcal{U}$ – patterns of w-similarity classes of universals, considered as functions of w – become the individuals ("substances") in the basis of $\mathcal{SA}$, as desired.

That was all pretty straightforward. What is not so evident is that the new $\mathcal{SA}$ possible worlds will match up with the old $\mathcal{U}$ ones. In the simplest, monadic case, the connection is as follows: let a_w be a's w-similarity class according to $\mathcal{U}$. $\mathcal{SA}$'s "states of affairs"[7] will then be its *constituent sequences* $\langle R^n, a_1, \ldots, a_n \rangle$ (in the sense of Barwise and Perry (1983: 53); cf. ch. 3 n. 8); in the monadic case $\langle F, a \rangle$. An $\mathcal{SA}$ world w' is then a set of states of affairs (constituent sequences) such that

$$\langle F, a \rangle \in w' \text{ iff } F \in a_w,$$

and similarly for polyadic universals R^n, where w is a $\mathcal{U}$ world.[8]

5C6   Substance–attribute to tropes

Next, take a substance–attribute structure $\mathcal{SA}$. Its constituent sequences become the "tropes" of a new trope structure $\mathcal{T}$. Furthermore, we define metarelations between constituent sequences as follows. They are "like" when their first element is the same. They 1-concur if their second element is the same. They 2-concur if their third element is the same, and so on. (For i-concurrence, see §2B3.) That gives us the basis for a trope structure $\mathcal{T}$.

We want to make sure that instantiation is preserved in $\mathcal{T}$. Let a' be a's 1-concurrence equivalence class of tropes (a $\mathcal{T}$ individual) and let F' be F's likeness class of tropes (a $\mathcal{T}$ property). Clearly a'

will contain $\langle F, a \rangle$, as will F'. Thus $a' \bigcirc F'$ and $\S F'a' = \langle F, a \rangle$ (notation: §2B8). If $\langle F, a \rangle \in w$, then $\S F'a' \in w$, the definition of $\mathcal{T}$ instantiation in w (§2B9).

5C7 Tropes to substance–trope

To get a substance–trope structure $\mathcal{ST}$ out of a trope structure $\mathcal{T}$ is almost a matter of course, for all the components of an $\mathcal{ST}$ basis are available in $\mathcal{T}$. However, if we take it as a defining characteristic of $\mathcal{ST}$ that its individuals *not* be bundles of tropes, then we shall have to find something other than $\mathcal{T}$'s "individuals" (trope bundles) to do the job. The kernels or representatives of §2C2 seem cut out for the task. This would make an individual a special kind of trope – not quite what substance–attribute theorists had in mind, perhaps, but good enough for the basis of a substance–trope structure $\mathcal{ST}$.

5C8 Substance–trope back to particularism

Finally, a substance–trope structure $\mathcal{ST}$ provides individuals in its basis and constructed possible worlds. (They are constructed combinatorially as sets of tropes or, alternatively, sets of states of affairs.) That suffices for the basis of a particularist structure $\mathcal{P}$.

With that we have come full circle. Each type of structure can be based on any of the other four types by traveling part-way around the circle. This establishes an approximate equivalence among the five types of structure, and hence among the five ontologies. This is a very important result, too little heeded by metaphysicians who like to argue for or against universals, nominalism, tropes, etc. Perhaps the wisest counsel would be Carnap's principle of tolerance: acknowledge the bulges in the carpet. But notwithstanding the rough equivalence, there are angles from which the ontologies differ in appeal. Let us take them up one by one.

5C9 Substance–trope theory

This is the view favored by Martin and Armstrong (when wearing his tropophile hat; cf. §1A8; ch. 1 n. 18) that we need both basic individuals as well as tropes to characterize them. The theory suffers from two defects, in my opinion. First, it is ontologically prodigal. Each individual will have its unique bundle of tropes anyway, which could very well take over the work of the individual "itself". All that is saved by the refusal of this move is the assumption of a concurrence relation: systematic bundling gives way to arbitrary bundling. I suspect that the reluctance to embrace bundles is really a survival of a historically deeply ingrained conviction that substance is basic. The second defect of substance–trope theory is that is cannot, on its own terms, account for universals. As Armstrong points out (1989b: 119f), it must have recourse to a relation of likeness (exact resemblance) among tropes. The result will be a bundle theory of universals perched atop a refusal of a bundle theory of individuals. Stranger positions have been taken by philosophers, but perhaps with more reason.

5C10   Substance and attribute

As we saw in §5C2, this view is already recommended to some extent by considerations of parsimony. It may also be the view that is closest to common sense. Most people, I suspect, think of the world as made up of things. If pressed, they will readily agree that the properties and relations of those things also make a difference. So far, so good. But even at the common-sense level, it is hard to persuade people (or beginning students anyway) that properties are simply more *things*, on a par with shoes and ships. Among philosophers, it is natural to account properties and relations *abstract*. Their metaphysical status is often felt to be problematic, by comparison with that of concrete things. The substance-attribute view fails to address this asymmetry, as Ramsey pointed out (1931). Of course, refraining to construct universals out of something else doesn't necessarily disqualify the substance-attribute advocate from theorizing about universals. But such a construction, if possible, would shed light on the prima facie problematic status of universals.

5C11   Universalism[9]

This is an elegant approach to basic ontology that goes back to Plato. I have adjusted it to contemporary concerns by including several different similarity relations of universals as so many different possible worlds (cf. Bacon 1988: §§12, 51). These relations are, of course, themselves universals (first-level as opposed to ground-level). Thus, in a sense, universalism is a one-category ontology. To get individuals, this theory forms similarity classes or bundles of ground-level universals. The single category is to some degree illusory, however, for deleting the lowest level (individuals) of a type hierarchy doesn't materially alter the structure of the hierarchy, unless it be finite. And even if it is, it could be argued that first-level relations are as categorially different from ground-level universals as the latter are from individuals. "Universals" of the lowest level in effect become new individuals. The main drawback to this theory, as to the substance–attribute view, is that it furnishes no analysis of what a property or a universal is. And unlike the substance–attribute view, its basic entities are farther removed from common sense. As it stands, universalism is somewhat weaker than the trope theory of chapter 7 below. (It is closer to the substance model-structures of §4B2.) The possible worlds developed in §7A8 are subtler, furnishing a basis for state-of-affairs concepts and relation-concepts. A similar extension of universalism might be possible. It is a framework worth exploring.

5C12 Particularism[10]

This is trope theory's most formidable rival. It is the approach familiar from the model theory of classical and modal logic. Individuals are primitive, as in common sense. Following Kanger and Kripke, properties are represented by classes of individuals in extensional contexts, by functions from worlds to classes in intensional contexts. For relations, the classes become classes of n-tuples. This approach has been enormously successful as a basis for exploring the comparative conditions for semantic completeness of various systems of logic. The Kanger–Kripke conception of properties has shed light on their metaphysical uses. Although this conception has in the end proved inadequate, there is some reason to hope that it might be refined. As it stands, the particularist approach yields too few properties for hyperintensional contexts, but too many for explicating supervenience (cf. Bacon forthcoming). Be that as it may, the ultimate difficulty with particularism is that it takes possible worlds as basic. These are even more remote from common sense and worrisome to philosophers than universals. (In a limited semantic context, valuations can make do as possible worlds, but not in general.)

5C13   Trope theory: a slight nod

Although trope theory is not strikingly more elegant or parsimonious than the above ontological approaches, its modest advantages are attractive. Of its two basic categories, one comprises things of a kind with which we are all acquainted (relatings, tropes); the other is neatly homogeneous (similarity relations). (Ultimately other categories are needed, of course; see §5A9.) The items it constructs (apart from individuals) are just the sort of things that seem to cry out for the clarification such a construction offers; namely, properties, relations of individuals, and possible worlds (not to mention states of affairs and (hyper)propositions). Trope theory makes a little more sense of things than the other four ontologies. This judgment is a little impressionistic, to be sure, and I cannot expect everyone to share it. Apart from the relative elegance of the theory and the epistemic accessibility of its elements, the proof will be in the eating. So let's turn to four applications: the use of tropes in accounts of time, belief, causation, and duty.

6

Taking Time

6A Tropes' Times

6A1 Times as individuals?

Many tropes have times: it makes sense to ask when they occur or obtain. What are these times? Certain possible answers may be disposed of at the outset. First, it might be suggested that times are ground-level individuals. On such a view, many apparently n-place predicates are really $(n + 1)$-place, with an added time parameter. The difficulty with this in our scheme is that there's no natural place for the time parameter. If we put it first, then atemporal tropes will have to be assigned some arbitrary dummy "time" aspect. If we put it last, no one aspect can be specified (since we don't know a priori the highest polytrope degree, and there may be none.) We could put it arbitrarily in the middle somewhere, but that seems artificial. And even if these housekeeping details could somehow be managed, temporal concurrence would become an equivalence relation, simultaneity, on which the theory of relativity throws doubt. It doesn't look like a good idea to treat times as individuals.

6A2 Times as ground-level properties or tropes?

If times aren't particulars, perhaps they're universals of some sort. Could they be ground-level properties, sets of like tropes? This would be analogous to Campbell's treatment of places, which he credits to Michael Shepanski (1990: 69, 177 n. 8). According to this view, for the Temple to fall on the 9th of Av, 70, would involve the Temple's fall concurring with the Temple's being on the 9th of Av. The trouble is that the Temple was at many other times too. If they are Temple tropes, they too concur with the Temple's fall. The Temple must have been falling all along, and Titus (and even Nebuzaradan) could have spared themselves the trouble. But of course that's ridiculous. Times are neither ground-level properties nor tropes thereof.

6A3 Times as first-level properties of tropes?

It makes some sense to take times as properties of tropes. Such an approach would be somewhat analogous to the treatment of dates in tense logic. Notice, though, that metaphysically properties of tropes are on a par with relations of tropes, i.e. metarelations. And as there are many, many times, there would be many, many such properties. It would be desirable to find an economical way of generating them, as the one metarelation of likeness generates all the universals.

6A4 Atomism?

Trope philosophers seem to have a weakness for a kind of physical atomism. (I don't mean "logical" or metaphysical atomism as in §1C4f.) As long as we're thinning properties down to their instances, tropes, it comes to seem natural and desirable to localize the tropes as much as possible, to take them as more or less punctiform, as particle-instants. In contrast, when I give examples of tropes like Phryne's loveliness or the Temple's fall, I mean them straight, not as rough heuristic stand-ins for this quark's strangeness or that proton's decay. Accordingly, I take the times at which tropes obtain to be *intervals*. Phryne's loveliness lasted some years; the fall of the Temple took several days. For many purposes, such intervals need not be sharply demarcated. The important thing is that it make sense to say that one wholly preceded the other. We can then borrow a method of Russell's for constructing instants out of the tropes occupying the intervals (1914: 93–6; 1936).[1]

6A5 Precedence

If a trope s takes place wholly before t, i.e. s is over before t begins, then I shall say that s precedes t, or $s < t$. Precedence is a third metarelation (counting concurrence as one). As one would expect, it is irreflexive, asymmetric, and transitive. It's not assumed that all tropes stand in the precedence relation; those that do are *temporal* tropes. Assessing precedence may again involve relativistic problems of simultaneity at the microlevel, but this need not vitiate the objectivity of everyday judgments about what came first, up to a degree of accuracy satisfactory to historians and the law courts.

6A6 Time lines

Two temporal tropes need not be temporally related: neither need precede the other. Precedence is thus not connected. But if a pair of tropes is connected by a chain of $<$ and $>$ links, they will be in the same time line.[2] More precisely, let

$$s <> t =_{df} s < t \lor t < s.$$

The ancestral $<>_*$ of this relation is *cotemporality*, temporal relatedness.[3] Cotemporality is an equivalence relation on temporal tropes. As such, it partitions the temporal tropes into tight bundles (equivalence classes). These bundles are *time lines*, each ordered by precedence.

6A7 Temporal overlap: instants

Cotemporal tropes s, t *overlap* temporally when neither precedes the other:

$$s \sqcap t =_{df} {\sim}(s <> t).$$

It is for this relation that the connectives 'while' and 'during' are sometimes used, depending on subtleties of verb aspect. (They can also express temporal inclusion.) Russell's term for this relation is 'simultaneity' (1914: 94; 1936: 347). Overlapping is a similarity relation (reflexive and symmetric but not necessarily transitive). As such it sorts the tropes on a given time line into loose bundles (similarity classes), maximal classes of temporally overlapping tropes. These overlap-bundles are Russell's *instants* (1914: 94f; 1936: 350).

6A8   Kernels: time points

Although we could use instants just as they are, it is a little easier to think in terms of their representatives. In general, loose bundles may have no unique representatives, because they may intersect. But it sometimes happens that loose bundles have *kernels* (cf. ch. 1 n. 23). A kernel of an instant is such that any two tropes overlapping it overlap each other. Equivalently, the elements of the instant are just the overlappers of the kernel. The assumption that there are instants (§6A4) is equivalent to the assumption that there are kernels occupying them. I assume, with Russell,[4] that instants have kernels. These can represent the instants. An instant may have more than one kernel, but as they overlap just the same tropes, one can serve as well as the other. One only is to be selected as representative. The kernels representing instants will be our *time points*. Unlike instants, time points fall within the field of $<$.

6A9   Time series, intervals, and times

Although precedence is not connected on tropes, temporal tropes, cotemporal tropes, or cotemporal kernels, it *is* connected on cotemporal time points. For overlapping points will be identical (uniqueness of representatives). Thus, where s and t are cotemporal points,

$$s \neq t \rightarrow \sim(s \sqcap t).$$

By the definition of $\sqcap$ (§606) we get connectedness:

$$s \neq t \rightarrow s <> t.$$

Thus on cotemporal points, precedence is an irreflexive, asymmetric, transitive, connected relation, a *serial ordering*. The set of time points on a given time line as serially ordered by precedence is a *time series*. A time *interval*, closed or open, is a non-empty set of consecutive time points: any point between two points is included.[5] Precedence extends from tropes to intervals in an obvious way, which will be taken for granted from here on. Finally, the *time of* a trope t is the interval it occupies, the set of time points it overlaps:[6]

$$\mathbb{T}(t) =_{\text{df}} \{s: \text{time point } s \ \& \ s \sqcap t\}.$$

("Time point" was defined in §6A8.) As one would expect, it turns out that

$$s \sqcap t \text{ iff } \mathbb{T}(s) \bigcirc \mathbb{T}(t).$$

For if cotemporal tropes s and t overlap, then they belong to a common instant (since instants have kernels). Thus they overlap a common kernel or time point, which is likewise common to their times. Conversely, if two tropes' times have a time point in common, it will be a kernel overlapping both tropes, so they will overlap each other.

Roughly speaking, the time of a state of affairs is the union of the times of its component tropes. More precisely, the time of a simple state of affairs is the time of its trope:

$$\mathbb{T}([t]) = \mathbb{T}(t).$$

The time of a negative state of affairs is the same as that of its positive:

$$\mathbb{T}(\sim p) = \mathbb{T}(p).$$

(In a world where p isn't, p's time is when it isn't, not all the times before and after p.) And the time of a dyadic compound is the union of its components' times:

$$\mathbb{T}(p \ \& \ q) = \mathbb{T}(p \lor q) = \mathbb{T}(p) \cup \mathbb{T}(q).$$

The time of a state of affairs, unlike a trope, will not necessarily be an interval. The precedence relation can nevertheless be easily extended from intervals to state-of-affairs times and thence to the states of affairs themselves. I leave aside for now other sorts of compound states of affairs.

6A10 Dates, gaps, and clocks

Depending on the number of tropes, a time series may be correlated with the rational or the real numbers and the time intervals of tropes measured. Taking the measure of a standard trope's interval as our unit, we are now in a position to establish a calendar and start measuring the "minutes" or "years" from some chosen origin, assigning dates.

It might look as though the possibility is left open that some instant in the physical sense might be empty, with no trope as its time point. While such temporal gaps are not absolutely ruled out, remember that the set T includes possible tropes as well as actual ones. A temporal gap in our world would quite likely be plugged by a trope in some other possible world. That it is indeed so seems a reasonable metaphysical hypothesis.

It may seem implausible to recognize time gaps in the actual world. It might be asked, "How could we tell?", since we could only notice the passage of tropes: if there were gaps, how could we detect them? But that smacks of verificationism, making physics dependent upon epistemology. Instead, the modern conception of time seems to presuppose that there's always something happening, that every instant is occupied. Practically speaking, we make it so by keeping busy and building clocks, but obviously nature has put a clock there already. (Our most accurate clocks, atomic clocks, have a natural escapement at their heart that needs no winding. Nor do sundials, which go off only during sustaining tropes of cloud movement.)

We have now reconstructed time in trope theory on the basis of four assumptions. (1) Some tropes are temporal: it makes sense to say that one wholly precedes another in time. (2) Instants, or overlapping-similarity-classes, have kernels. (3) The time series is not dense. (4) There are no tropeless stretches of physical time.

6B Continuants and Temporal Unity

6B1 All individuals temporal?

Individuals are made up of tropes, we said, bundled and strung together into chains. Some of those tropes will be temporal, ordered by $<$ and timed and perhaps even dated. It would be tempting to define a temporal individual as one containing a temporal trope. But it seems that practically anything, temporal or not, can stand in temporal relations. For example, the number seven might be considered a timeless individual; yet its being my favorite integer is temporal. If you think seven is a universal, substitute your own example x. It will probably still make sense to speak of someone's liking x. It begins to look as though any individual might contain temporal tropes.

6B2 Essential tropes and lifetimes

What seems to be called for here is some distinction between the essential and the accidental tropes making up an individual. An essential trope t of a is an existing element of some one aspect of a in every possible world where a exists:

$$t \in \mathscr{E}(a) \text{ iff } \exists\, i \forall w \in W(\mathrm{E}_w a \rightarrow t \in a_w^i \,\&\, t \in k_w).^7$$

(we could consider attenuating the metaphysical necessity here to physical or some other mode of necessity.) $\mathscr{E}(a)$ is the *essence* of a, the set of all its essential tropes. The temporal subset $\mathscr{E}_\tau(a)$ is the set of essential *temporal* tropes of a. These are assumed to be cotemporal. a is then *temporal* iff $\mathscr{E}_\tau(a) \neq \Lambda$. The time of a, its *lifetime*, consists of the times of its essential temporal tropes:

$$\mathbb{T}(a) = \cup\mathbb{T}``\mathscr{E}_\tau(a).$$

6B3 Intermittent individuals?

Like $\mathbb{T}(t)$ (6A9, n. 6), it looks as though $\mathbb{T}(a)$ might fail to be an interval: a might be an intermittent or temporally gappy individual, like Brigadoon or a token of a melody (Sellars' example, 1962–3). I want to argue that intermittent individuals can be ruled out, however.

It's not clear that a melody ceases during its gaps or rests. Their length is usually as integral to the piece as that of the notes, and we feel the beeping of a watch during a rest as an intrusion. All this suggests that the gaps are part of the melody, not interruptions of it.

Brigadoon is, I suppose, metaphysically possible, although it's quite hard to think of similar examples in the actual world.[8] If we did encounter one, I suggest that we would treat successive Brigadoon-stages as distinct individuals. If we are prepared to count institutional dissolution as loss of existence, then a revived club or state, such as Israel,[9] would be an intermittent item, though not obviously an individual.

Yet, can't we make Brigadoon-like individuals any time we want just by taking two temporally separated objects a and b as parts of a larger whole $c = a + b$? That would be to *define c* as $a + b$, so that $a \P c$ and $b \P c$ in every possible world where a and b exist.[10] Being *ex hypothesi* temporal, a and b have essential temporal tropes and hence essences, making 'a' and 'b' very nearly rigid designators (rigid but not strongly rigid in Kripke's terms).[11] That makes 'c' equally rigid, and likewise 'a's being part of c'; i.e., $\S_u(a \P c) = \S_w(a \P c)$ for all $u, w \in W$ where a and b and therefore c exist. Thus $\S_a(a \P c)$ is an essential trope of c. It is also temporal, lasting as long as c does. So $\S_a(a \P c)$ bridges the supposed gap between a and b, preventing c from winking out then, and $c = a + b$ is not intermittent after all. The same would be true of Brigadoon if we incorporated its centennial existential winks into an ongoing village. I conclude that every temporal individual is a *continuant*.

6B4 Change

There are several ways for a continuant to change. One of its temporal tropes may itself be an instance of change, a *dynamic* trope, such as a bird's flight, a baby's cry, or a philosopher's surprise. Another kind of change occurs when one of the continuant's temporal tropes stops or starts within its lifetime.[12] In both cases, the trope involved may be essential or inessential, making for essential or inessential change. The latter need not be mere "Cambridge" change. Dying my hair or learning Finnish is an inessential but not a Cambridge change in me. (It appears that Cambridge changes are all relational, but not vice versa. I don't know how to define Cambridge change.) Thus changes in individuals are changes in their tropes: essential or inessential, dynamic or beginning or ending.

6B5 Identity through time?

There is something odd about asking what makes for the identity of a continuant through time. To begin with, it's not clear that 'identity' is being used in its basic sense. Identity is a reflexive relation, but the question can hardly be what makes an object *self-identical* (through time or *ut nunc*). Of *course* Shirley Temple Black is identical with Shirley Temple. And of *course* the Congress-woman stage is not identical with the child-star stage. Is this the problem: how can the stages be different but the continuant one? If so, we might speak better of temporal *unity*.

6B6 Modal analogues

In recent decades, a modal analogue has been developed of the problem of identity through time: the problem of identity across possible worlds. Three approaches have crystallized. (1) Take the identity for granted: put literally the same particulars in each possible world (cf. our substance-modelings, §4A2). (2) Construe

"identity" from world to world as straightness of world-lines
(§§4A5ff). (3) Replace identity by Lewis's counterpart relation
(1979). It will have been evident that I don't fully maintain a
parallel between time and possible worlds. It is nevertheless
helpful to consider the temporal analogues of (1)–(3). The analogue
of (3) would start with object-stages and then follow out the
temporal counterparts. This is rather unsatisfactory, as the
counterpart relation is not transitive, and its ancestral is too
sweeping. Thus a stage could belong to more than one continuant
on this approach. This would at least make identity through time
a problem. The temporal analogue of (1) would assume individuals
stretched out in time. That would amount to ignoring the problem.

6B7   *Straightness and temporal threads*

The approach I have taken is closest to (2). A thing's time is given
by its essential temporal tropes, as a straight world-line is determined by a recurring transworld trope. The two are connected, in
that an essential temporal trope in a is almost enough to make the
concept of a a straight world-line. But what unifies a's essential
temporal tropes? Nothing more nor less than that they are tropes
of a. And what makes them tropes of a? Concurrence and collimation (§2B6). These are the foundation of a's temporal unity.

The straightness analogy can be carried a step further. A
straight world-line has one trope continuing through all its values
(§4A7), which we might call its transworld thread. Similarly, some
continuants will have one or more *temporal threads*[13] t such that

$$t \in \mathscr{E}_\tau(a) \ \& \ [\mathbb{T}(t) = \mathbb{T}(a)].$$

Such a continuant possesses a higher degree of unity than a temporal essence. It has at least one essential trope coterminous with
its lifetime. Let us call such a continuant *threaded*. Threaded
continuants range from stones to people. Indeed, it is conceivable,
though doubtful, that every temporal individual is threaded. Thus
the threaded continuant, with its "subtle parts" (Williams), has
what Theseus's ship lacks in the way of gross parts: a lifelong
lasting component.

Threads, I suggest, make for "identity through time" in the strong sense of that mysterious phrase. An individual is "identical over time" if it has a temporal thread. But this may be felt to beg the question. What makes the temporal thread, a trope, identical over time? To which I answer, all explanation must stop somewhere, and this is a good place to stop. Every trope, temporal or not, is just the trope it is. Overlapping several time points does not break up the trope's unity but rather presupposes it.

6B8 Personal identity

The above considerations apply to persons as well as to anything else. A person will have "identity through time" only if he has some temporal threads, some lifetime tropes. Perhaps those tropes should also be essential and sufficient for personhood. Do we have any such threads? It seems to me that we do. Indeed, my personhood itself is an essential lifetime trope of mine. Unless it is too complex to count as a simple trope, it can serve nicely as the connecting thread of my life, of me. If this seems too easy, again, just where is it sensible for explanation to stop?

6B9 The level of precedence

As has been made clear (§§5A4, 6A5), temporal precedence is a metarelation, a first-level relation between tropes, not a ground-level relation of individuals. As such, it lends itself most naturally to bundling as a bundle of hypertropes (cf. ch. 1 n. 13) in the context of a trope cascade (§5A3). I have already expressed reservations about the latter, as wanting metaphysical plausibility. The only other way to get precedence (or some other basic temporal relation) by bundling would be to make it a ground-level relation. But then it would be unclear how to date tropes and states of affairs. We're left with temporal precedence as a basic metarelation, probably an atom, possibly a bundle of hypertropes.

7

Belief

7A   Objects of Belief

7A1   *Belief as a relation*

Is belief relational? The very phrase "object of belief" suggests
that it is. There are, to be sure, notorious difficulties with the
various attempts that have been made to construe belief as relation. To my mind, these are outweighed by semantic considerations, foremost among them the desideratum of *compositionality* of
'believes'-contexts. The meaning of 'Jo believes that p' should
somehow be a function of the meanings of 'Jo', 'believes', and
'that p'. This does not rule out the possibility of construing 'that
p' as an "adverbial" modifier of an intransitive verb 'believes'. But
it does seem to militate in favor of an accusative construction. Our
language treats belief as a relation between a subject and an object
indicated by a 'that'-clause. Can we hope to do better by turning
our back on this entrenched bit of "folk psychology"? Previous
attempts have not been encouraging. Let us stick with the "folk"
and try a relational account of belief once again.

7A2   *Its terms*

If belief is a relation, what does it relate? Two different kinds of
thing: as subject (in the first argument-place), a person or con-
scious being (such as an animal). In the second position (second

argument-place), a thing believed, as expressed by a 'that' clause. Sellars used to call these "believees" (1962–3). He explained that this was one of the main purposes for which the term *'proposition'* had come to be used in contemporary philosophy. (The other main use is for 'sentence meaning'.) What then, is a propposition, a believee?

7A3   *Propositions as states of affairs*

The reader who's got this far will be familiar enough with modern theories of propositions, so it would be pointless for me to review them here in detail. The Frege–Church–Carnap–Kripke conception has been the most fruitful and the most influential, even if it has proved inadequate for believees. According to this view, a proposition is a set of possible worlds or, equivalently, a function from possible worlds to truth-values. This is what I am here calling a *state of affairs*. The trouble with states of affairs as believees is that they are not fine-grained enough: their identity conditions are still too coarse. Logically equivalent states of affairs are identical, yet one can believe the one and not the other. For example, these two are consistent:

> Jo believes that she has two eyes.
> Jo doesn't believe that she has an even prime number of eyes.

But unless we allow *impossible worlds* where the laws of arithmetic break down, this pair would be inconsistent on a state-of-affairs reading.

Since each trope corresponds to a simple state of affairs (§3D5), tropes are likewise inadequate as believees, and for the same reason. And for the compound tropes that would be needed, the closest thing we have are just compound states of affairs (see part 3D).

7A4   *Propositions as heaven sets*

The use of impossible worlds has been explored by Cresswell (1972: 4; 1973: 40f) and others (see references in Cressewell 1973:

40nn.). There Cresswell introduces the notion of a *heaven*, a set of states of affairs (in our sense), or of proto-propositions, as he calls them. Every possible world corresponds to a heaven, its world-heaven, but not necessarily vice versa. It is these heavens that are not world-heavens that play a role in Cresswell's theory rather like that of impossible worlds. But by constructing them thus step by step out of possible worlds, Cresswell avoids positing weird worlds *ad hoc* just to cater for vagaries of illogic. Finally, Cresswell defines a proposition as a set of heavens. Two sentences are logically equivalent if they stand for the same state of affairs (proto-proposition), *synonymous* if they express the same proposition. Just what actually makes for synonymy depends on the choice of heavens for an intended model, a job for semanticists rather than metaphysicians. As believees, propositions are called for whose sentential expressions will be interchangeable in 'believes' contexts *salva veritate*. Cresswell's framework makes a place for such propositions without telling us just where that place is.

7A5   Surfeit of propositions

Cresswell's scheme, which he says he worked out partly in discussion with David Lewis, is very interesting and suggestive. I wonder, though, if it doesn't yield *too many* propositions. Where T is the set of tropes (basic particular situations), the set of Cresswellian propositions will be $2^{2^{2^{2^T}}}$. That means that if there is just one trope, there will be 65,536 propositions! Indeed, even if there are *no* tropes, we still get 16 propositions. It's hard to imagine what to do with all these. The acknowledged ultimate extreme in the individuation of believees has been to assign a different proposition to each sentence. But it strains credulity to suppose that 65,536 nonsynonymous sentences could be formulated to talk meaningfully about a one-trope world and an empty world (the two worlds in 2^T for singleton T). The Razor seems in order here.

7A6   Propositions as state-of-affairs concepts

Cresswell has pointed the way. Let's see if we can simplify his scheme somewhat while still following his lead. He introduced heavens and heaven sets (his propositions) because states of affairs proved too coarse-grained. But there is another way to refine them. Just as 'believes' looks relational, so does 'fears'. Yet we recognize that objects of fear are intentional, so that in

Jo fears the Erlkönig,

the grammatical object 'the Erlkönig' occurs in a referentially opaque context. 'Fears' accordingly relates Jo not to any elf king, but to the Erlkönig-concept, in Church's sense of 'concept'.[2] I suggest construing

Jo believes that Tasman is tall

analogously. 'That Tasman is tall', we have recognized, stands for a trope or the corresponding state of affairs. But as it occurs here in an opaque context, 'believes' relates Jo not to a trope or a state of affairs, but to a state-of-affairs concept, a function from possible worlds to states of affairs.[3] These are what I will call *propositions*, the appropriate believees or objects of belief (and of various other propositional attitudes). Propositions in this sense are fine-grained enough. From a certain point of view, they can be seen as a special case of Cresswellian propositions, which, however, I suggested are too fine-grained. By comparison, if there is just one trope I get $2^{2^1 \cdot 2} = 16$ propositions,[4] as against Cresswell's 65,536.

7A7 Contingent likeness: attributes

Originally I took possible worlds simply to be sets of tropes (§§1B2, 1E6). Later I added a concurrence relation (§4A5), so that a possible world became a pair $\langle k, I \rangle$, consisting of a possible world k in the old sense, now called a world-core (actually, a set of trope singletons), and a concurrence relation I. Allowing I to help constitute a world makes the individuation of particulars variable from world to world. In the context of belief, it makes sense also to allow likeness to vary, for the believer might individuate properties differently according to world. Thus likeness, like concurrence, now becomes an external or contingent relation between tropes, capable of distinguishing one world from another. Though logically possible, worlds thus distinguished may or may not be doxastically accessible. With likeness relativized to worlds, properties and relations become world-bound. A given predicate may stand for one property in world α and another in world w. Thus there arise functions from worlds to properties, property-concepts or, as we might call them, *attributes*. In the polyadic case we get *relationships*, i.e. relation-concepts.

7A8   Possible worlds complicated

We arrive accordingly at a conception of possible worlds as triples $\langle k, h, I \rangle$ consisting of a world-core k, a likeness relation h, and a concurrence relation I. Where $w \in W$ is such a world, its components will also be referred to as k_w, h_w, and I_w. For most of our investigation of belief, however, we can forget about the complications of §3A5, which replaced world-cores and universals by their singleton sets and individuals' i-bundles by their power sets. Thus 'ι''' can be dispensed with in §§4B2, 4B5, and D^n_w is simply $\overrightarrow{I^n_w}$''T (the set of n-concurrence-in-w bundles of tropes).

7A9   Propositions as relations

A state of affairs, I said (§3D4), is a set of possible worlds, which is to say a function from worlds to truth-values. Accordingly, a proposition, a function from possible worlds to states of affairs, is simultaneously a dyadic function from worlds to truth-values, or a dyadic relation between worlds, a set of world pairs.[5] Another way to describe this construction is that, in the now usual sense of 'proposition' (a world set), worlds are replaced by world pairs. This way of thinking of our relative propositions is particularly useful heuristically. Identical world pairs – those of the form $\langle w, w \rangle$ – play a role similar to that of Cresswell's classical worlds (1973: 40). And each relative proposition p determines a special associated state of affairs $p^=$, i.e. $\{w: p(w, w)\}$, the set of worlds where p is true. '$p(u, w)$' or '$u \in p_w$' says that the state of affairs which p assigns to w obtains in u.

7A10   Simple propositions

A simple state of affairs $[t]$ is defined as the set of all worlds containing a given trope t (§3D5). In view of §7A8, we must now say, containing t in their core:

$$[t] = \{u \in W: t \in k_u\}.$$

Now, t may itself be given in the context of simple instantiation of a syntropic relation (cf. §4A6). It may, for example, be John's loving Mary in w,

$$\S L^2_{\,w} j_w m_w.$$

(In contrast to §§3A2, 4B6, $L^2_{\,w}$ is now an h_w similarity class comprising w's lovings, existent and nonexistent. This complication arises from the relativization of likeness to worlds in §7A7.) Let us abbreviate this to

$$\S_w L^2 jm.$$

By syntropy and plenitude this must be a proper description of a unique trope. It accordingly determines a simple state of affairs

$$[\S_w L^2 jm].$$

But which state of affairs it determines will be a function of w:

$$\lambda w [\S_w L^2 jm].$$

Such a function is a *simple* proposition: it assigns each world a simple state of affairs.

With propositions in hand as the appropriate objects of belief, we proceed to the analysis of the structure of the belief relation itself.

7B   The Structure of Belief

7B1   Hintikka's doxastic logic

In the development of modal logic over the last thirty years, the most familiar approach to belief, as originated by Hintikka (1962: 48), is to treat it just like any other modality, e.g. necessity (cf. ▣ in §4C7):

$$|BA|_w = \text{T iff } \forall u(w\Delta u \to |A|_u = \text{T}),$$

where $|\ \ |$ is a valuation on an appropriate model-structure that includes a dyadic relation Δ of doxastic accessibility. Translated from the semantics of sentences into the metaphysics of states of affairs, with '$\mathscr{D}$' for '$\overset{\leftarrow}{\Delta}$', this becomes

$$Bp = \{w: \mathscr{D}(w) \subseteq p\}.$$

The world w's doxastic accessibility sphere, $\mathscr{D}(w)$, is itself a state of affairs (proposition, as we would usually say) included in or implying p. What state of affairs? The conjunction of all the subject's beliefs at w, in effect. (The apparent circularity of characterizing 'B' by means of '$\mathscr{D}$' is like that of characterizing '&' by means of 'and': structural analysis, not definition is intended.)

7B2   Logical omnicredence

The notorious defect of this approach is that it makes belief closed under logical consequence:

> If $A \mathrel{\Vdash} C$ then $BA \mathrel{\Vdash} BC$
> If $p \subseteq q$ then $Bp \subseteq Bq$.

Actual belief, of course, doesn't work like that; we are not always perfectly logical in our beliefs. And a decision to let 'B' stand for *rational* belief or "ideal belief" just changes the subject. The analogous difficulty with knowledge is called "logical omniscience"; here we may accordingly speak of "logical omnicredence".

7B3   The substitutivity paradox

Frege taught us that in referentially opaque or intensional contexts, names may in general replace each other only if they have the same (ordinary) sense (intension) (1892). Modern reconstructions of Frege have tended to follow Carnap (1947: 27) in making logical equivalence the identity criterion for senses. Frege almost certainly had a stricter criterion in mind, and Carnap points out the need (1947: 124). Following Cresswell (1975), contexts such as belief-contexts which require such a stricter criterion are accordingly sometimes called "hyperintensional". Consider Quine's example (1960: 145):

(1)   Tom believes that Cicero denounced Catiline.
(2)   Cicero is Tully.
(3)   ∴ Tom believes that Tully denounced Catiline.

This is invalid because 'believes . . .' in (1) is an opaque context, and (2) merely gives 'Cicero' and 'Tully' the same referent, not the same sense. (Such names are not assumed to be rigid: §4B4.) That being so, 'Cicero denounced Catiline' and 'Tully denounced Catiline' likewise express different senses, different propositions. Now replace (2) and (3) by

(2')   'Cicero denounced Catiline' is logically equivalent
        to 'Catiline was denounced by Cicero'.[6]
(3')   ∴ Tom believes that Catiline was denounced by Cicero.

If logical equivalence is sufficient for sameness of sense, then the resulting argument should be valid, as it pretty clearly is not. (1) could be true while (3') was false – unless (3') be taken as a simple paraphrase of (1). But that would amount to a *transparent* reading of the belief context. On the primary, opaque reading a very dim Tom could believe the one and not the other.[7] One response to this situation would be to maintain the hyperintensionality of opaque belief. Another would be to deny that the logical equivalence (2′) gives the two sentences the same sense. They stand for the same state of affairs, but they don't express the same *proposition* in our sense (cf. §7A6 above). They are not, so to speak, rigid designators of states of affairs. The substitution argument involving (2′) thus fails for essentially Frege's reasons, provided we drop Frege's assumption that sentences refer to truth-values (cf. 7A6 n. 3). Alternatively, we could recognize in our propositions the *hyperintensions* of sentences. (The term is due to Cresswell 1975.) The moral I wish to draw from this consideration of the substitutivity paradox is that in the theory of belief we should replace states of affairs by propositions.

7B4   *Belief propositions: truth conditions*

The usual doxastic accessibility relation, the Δ of §7B1, is dyadic (triadic if the believer be taken into account). If p there is recon-strued as a proposition, rather than a state of affairs, Δ becomes a *tetradic* relation among worlds, propositions themselves being dyadic:

$$\mathrm{B}p = \{v{,}w\colon \forall uy[v\Delta_w uy \rightarrow p(u, y)]\}.$$

Defining

$$\mathscr{D}_w(v) =_{\mathrm{df}} \{u{,}y\colon v\Delta_w uy\},$$

we have, equivalently,

$$\mathrm{B}p = \{v{,}w\colon \mathscr{D}_w(v) \subseteq p\}.$$

$\mathscr{D}_w(v)$ is in effect the conjunction of all propositions the subject believes at $\langle v, w \rangle$, i.e. such that his believing them at w obtains in v. This tells us what proposition Bp will be for an arbitrary proposition p. It is easily translated into a truth condition for belief sentences:

$$|\mathrm{B}A|_w^v = \mathrm{T} \text{ iff } \forall uy(v\Delta_w uy \rightarrow |A|_y^u = \mathrm{T}),$$

i.e. $\mathscr{D}_w(v) \subseteq |A|$.

In place of '$|A|^v_w = \mathrm{T}$', we may write '$v \in |A|_w$' or simply '$v|A|w$'.

7B5 Entailment and implication

At least two different relations of conditionality between propositions, or sentences, may now be distinguished:

Entailment: $p \Vvdash q$ iff $p \subseteq q$;

$\quad A \Vvdash C$ iff $|A| \subseteq |C|$,

$\quad$ i.e. $\forall vw(|A|^v_w = \mathrm{T} \to |C|^v_w = \mathrm{T})$.

Implication: $p \Vdash q$ iff $p^= \subseteq q^=$;

$\quad A \Vdash C$ iff $|A|^= \subseteq |C|^=$,

$\quad$ i.e. $\forall w(|A|^w_w = \mathrm{T} \to |C|^w_w = \mathrm{T})$,

where $p^= =_{\mathrm{df}} \{w: p(w, w)\}$ (§7A9). Entailment is the stricter relation: it entails implication but not vice versa. A proposition p or a sentence A is true in a world if its associated state of affairs $p^=$ or $|A|^=$ obtains there. Thus implication is truth-preservation, logical consequence (cf. §7B10). Co-entailment is propositional identity; and co-implication, logical equivalence. Thus we should expect the former but not the latter to support substitution in belief-contexts. Indeed, it is immediately clear from the above definitions that $\mathrm{B}p \subseteq \mathrm{B}q$ if $p \subseteq q$ but not necessarily if $p^= \subseteq q^=$. By the same token, if $v|\mathrm{B}A|w$ i.e. $\mathscr{D}_w(v) \Vvdash A$, and $A \Vvdash C$, then $v|\mathrm{B}C|w$ follows, but not from $A \Vdash C$. This, in outline, is the solution to logical omnicredence and to the substitutivity paradox for belief-sentences.

The solution is a bit of a letdown when we look for actual examples of entailment. This is a matter of application. In order for p to entail q, the state of affairs p_w must be included in q_w in all possible worlds w. If you could believe p but not q, then p does not entail q. It appears that only the most trivial, obvious implications will count as entailments; for example, perhaps

Jo is a daughter $\Vvdash$ Jo is a girl

but not

Jo is a sister $\models$ Jo is a sibling.

While this may seem rather unsatisfactory, it fits the behavior of "believes".

7B6   Nonrigid logical constants

I've identified logical consequence with implication, but it remains to be seen whether it indeed falls short of entailment. In §3D5 I defined the conjunction of two states of affairs as their intersection. It might seem natural to define the conjunction of two propositions similarly. If the conjunction of the states of affairs p_w and q_w (p and q being propositions) is $p_w \cap q_w$, it seems natural to equate this with $(p \cap q)_w$, making $p \cap q$ the conjunctive proposition. But then p & $q \models p$ and accordingly $B(A$ & $C) \models BA$: we are back with logical omnicredence again. To reject it is to recognize that our believer may not always have a perfect grip on conjunction and other logical concepts.

Against such a recognition, some would hold that one either has the concept of conjunction or one doesn't, all or nothing. For a believer who has the concept, of course $B(A$ & $C) \models BA$. And if he doesn't have the concept of conjunction, then $\sim B(A$ & $C)$. To grasp a logical constant is to get it right in one's belief contexts. The reason this plausible position is ultimately untenable for me is that there is no clear dividing line between obvious implications like A & $C \Vdash A$ and difficult ones like A & $\sim A \Vdash C$ or $(A \to C) \to A \Vdash A$. (For the contrary view, see R. and V. Routley 1975: 211, 204.) There are certainly many believers of whom these fail:

$$B(A \ \& \sim A) \Vdash BC$$

$$B((A \to C) \to A) \Vdash BA.$$

Rather than make *some* logical inferences automatic in belief contexts, but others a matter of contingent logical acumen, it seems more realistic to treat them all alike as fallible achievements, even by believers who have the concept of conjunction, negation, or the conditional.[8]

Thus, in some of our believer's doxastically accessible worlds y, '&' may not stand for $\cap$: $|\&|_y \neq \cap$. In the actual world α, on the other hand, the logical constants have their standard meaning: $|\&|_\alpha = \cap$, etc. This is not quite the same as the impossible-worlds approach, although it is similar. y is not an impossible world where conjunction acts up (refusing to commute, say), but a possible world with respect to which the believer misconstrues conjunction. He can equally well misconstrue other logical constants. The valuation of the logical constants, like that of other expressions, is thus relativized to worlds. They cease to be rigid "designators".

7B7   Reflexive standardization

In contexts like '$w|A$ & $C|$ w', however, where the compound proposition relates a world to itself, the connective '&' will receive its standard interpretation. More generally, where $\times$ is a nonmodal logical constant,

$$w \in |A \times C|_w \leftrightarrow w \in (|A|_w \ |X|_w \ |C|_w)$$
$$\rightarrow w \in (|A|_w \ |X|_\alpha \ |C|_w).$$

(Obvious adjustments are to be made for '$\sim$' and quantifiers.) I call this assumption the principle of *reflexive standardization*. Where $|X|_v \neq |X|_\alpha$, it is left open what $|X|_v$ may be; presumably some other connective or quantifier of the same category as $|X|_\alpha$. 'B' is not a logical constant, but it is similarly relativized to worlds by the subscript 'w' on 'Δ' (or '$\mathscr{D}$'). For cosmological necessity $\boxed{4}$, take §4D5 as defining R_α and $\mathscr{A}_\alpha$; in idiosyncratic belief worlds v, R_v may not be R_α. Otherwise, where

$$\boxed{4}p = \{v,w: \mathscr{A}_w(v) \subseteq p^= \},$$

we get

$$w \in |\boxed{4}A|_w \leftrightarrow \mathscr{A}_w(w) \subseteq |A|^=$$

$$\rightarrow \mathscr{A}_\alpha(w) \subseteq |A|^=$$

as a further instance of reflexive standardization.

7B8 Adequacy of this treatment

It should now be clear that belief is closed under entailment but not under implication or even logical equivalence:

> If $p \models q$ then $Bp \models Bq$.
> Not: if $p \Vdash q$ then $Bp \Vdash Bq$.
> Not: if $p \dashv\vdash q$ then $Bp \Vdash Bq$.

The second of these denies logical omnicredence. The third undercuts the substitutivity paradox for logical equivalents. Cosmological necessity, on the other hand, is closed under implication, as we would expect, but in a rather strong sense:

> If $p \Vdash q$ then $\boxed{4}p \models \boxed{4}q$.

The criteria of adequacy for a metaphysical account and a modal theory of belief are thus satisfied.

7B9 Doxastic world-line models

As a postscript to this part, I return to the question whether the $\Vdash$ of §7B5 really represents logical consequence. The latter is defined in terms of models. The appropriate models here will be doxastic world-line models, as extended from §4A5. Such a model is a septuple $M = \langle T, H, \mathcal{J}, K, \Delta, \alpha, |\ \ |\rangle$, where for each $h \in H$, $\langle T, h, \mathcal{J}, K, \alpha \rangle$ is a world-line model structure (§4A5), except that now the actual world $\alpha \in W = K \times H \times \mathcal{J}$ (cf. §7A8). Δ is a tetradic relation on W. $|\ \ |$ is a valuation function assigning each meaningful expression X a referent $|X|_w$ in each world $w \in W$. I omit most of the details, including truth or valuation conditions for the various logical constants. Where 'L^2jm' is a simple sentence,

$$|L^2jm|_w = [\S_w L^2jm] = \{v\colon |j|^1_w \cap |m|^2_w \cap |L^2|_w \bigcirc v\}$$

(cf. §§4A6, 7A9). Compounds are handled as in §7B7, in keeping with reflexive standardization. For nonactual worlds w and logical constants X, $|X|_w$ will in general be arbitrary (contingent), except in reflexive contexts with another 'w' on the left. The doxastic world-line model M satisfies (is a model of) A iff $\alpha|A|\alpha$.

7B10   Logical implication

A logically implies C iff every model of A is a model of C; i.e.,

$$\alpha|A|\alpha \to \alpha|C|\alpha$$

for every $M = \langle \ldots, \alpha, | \quad | \rangle$ as above. Now, to every world $w \in W$ there will correspond a model $M_w = \langle \ldots, w, | \quad | \rangle$ which is just like M but with w in place of α, so that

$$w|A|w \to w|C|w$$

on M_w. But even if w were not the actual world, by reflexive standardization all logical constants in A and C would be treated the same as if w were actual. Thus $w|A|w \to w|C|w$ on M too, for every w. Accordingly $A \mathrel{\Vdash} C$ (on every M).

For the converse, if $A \mathrel{\Vdash} C$, we must make explicit what W and $|\ |$ are assumed, i.e. what model. It only makes sense to take the intended model, the model that is how things really are (even though we don't know exactly which one it is). Whatever the details, the intended model will have a possible world corresponding to each doxastic world-line model (if we have these right). Thus if C is true in every world in which A is true, then C will be true in every model in which A is true, and A will logically imply C. The upshot is that implication *is* logical implication, as maintained. This result buttresses the adequacy claimed in §7B8 for this approach to belief.

7C Loose Ends

7C1 De re *belief*

Throughout this chapter so far I have considered only "believes" contexts filled by a complete, self-contained sentence – *de dicto* contexts. These are sometimes also called opaque belief contexts, and the belief involved "opaque belief". Sometimes, however, a belief context may contain referentially transparent spots, with respect to which it is *de re*. If the *whole* context is such a spot, the belief is called by some "transparent belief". Under Quine's influence, there has been some feeling that transparent belief is less problematic, and that it would be desirable somehow to reduce opaque belief to transparent belief. This I consider totally unfeasible and misguided. *De dicto* belief is basic. *De re* belief contexts arise by quantifying in. This is made possible by straight world-lines (§4A7) as values of individual variables, as Thomason and Stalnaker have shown (1968). Thus:

The sheriff believes that Robin split Elwyn's arrow

in the *de re* sense that

The sheriff believes of Robin that he split Elwyn's arrow

is analyzed as

$\exists x \in \$$ (the sheriff believes that x split Elwyn's arrow & $x =$ Robin).

For contexts *de re* with respect to predicates, straight world-lines of universals would have to be delineated. An analogous task awaits us for adverbs and other parts of speech that can occur *de re* in otherwise intensional contexts.

7C2 *Tropes and the metaphysics of belief*

With the help of tropes, I have given an account of the objects of belief (part 7A). Recourse to tropes could have been avoided, with explanatory loss, by taking possible worlds as primitive. Thus, although this treatment of belief could have been developed independently of trope theory, it is grounded in the latter. The account of belief itself, as far as it goes, is primarily metaphysical. It is not just an analysis of belief *sentences*. The latter come in only with the valuations | |. To be sure, these are used in the treatment of the logical constants (§7B7), but even there reference to language could have been avoided, with some trouble.

7C3 Belief undefined

I have *not* said what belief is. I have characterized it in terms of doxastic accessibility Δ, and I haven't said what *that* is. A tetradic relation among possible worlds, it doesn't necessarily exhibit analogues of reflexivity or transitivity or other properties of relations. While the analysis in terms of Δ enables us to confront such problems as logical omnicredence, belief itself is surely a more familiar notion than Δ. It's not surprising that it should turn out to be basic, given its centrality to the functioning of the mind.

7C4 Logic of belief?

If B or Δ is primitive, then we might look to the logic of belief for further characterization. However, as I have set up the model theory, there is essentially *no* interesting logic of belief, no body of nontrivial logical truths or logical implications involving 'B' (cf. Cresswell 1972: 11). (This may explain the fatal attraction of logical omnicredence and similar *ignes fatui* for aspiring doxastic logicians.) And if an axiomatization of doxastic implications would be boring, obviously an axiomatization of doxastic entailments would be all the more so. Perhaps the best we can do in this vein is to note the logical place of belief in the network of propositional attitudes – such principles as:

j believes that $p \Vdash j$ doesn't doubt that p
j is disgusted that $p \Vdash j$ believes that p
j wonders whether $p \Vdash j$ doesn't believe that p
j wonders whether $p \Vdash j$ doesn't believe that $\sim p$
j hopes that $p \Vdash j$ believes that p is possible

and so forth. Whether we regard such principles as logical (as I do) or as synthetic a priori is of no great moment. They contribute significantly to the characterization of belief.

7C5 Logic of entailment?

Although I've given truth conditions for entailment (§7B5), I haven't axiomatized it. If we think of world-pairs for the moment simply as so many possible worlds, then it is evident that the pure-conditional fragment of the logic of entailment will be just like that of implication.[9] The difference comes in the logical constants, 'B', and many other notions about which the believer may have funny ideas. It may well then be asked (as Graham Priest has asked) how co-entailment differs from sameness of sentence as an identity criterion for believees. That extreme is not ruled out, but it is trivializing. My approach also permits the recognition of non-identical synonyms, and I do recognize them.

7C6 Belief tropes?

As examples of first-level tropes, we've had Socrates' wisdom, Othello's loving Desdemona, and many more denoted by nomi-nalized simple sentences. What about

> Jo's believing that Tasman is tall?

I've said that belief is a relation between a subject and a proposi-tion (§7A2), and that relations are bundles of like polytropes (§§1D3, 2B1). Those were ground-level relations, however, and first-level polytropes. Although similar constructions are possible at higher levels (§1B5), belief is not a single-level relation, but a heterogeneous one. It takes ground-level individuals as subjects but propositions as objects, to which we haven't even assigned a level. At any rate, propositions can scarcely be reckoned as individuals, given their multiplicity and their logical articulation. It's not just that they're complex or structured; we have recognized mereologically compound individuals (§3C). It's rather that their inner structure seems incomplatible with their being 2-concurrence bundles.

7C7   Constitutive circularity?

Consider

>   Jo's believing that she is a good girl.

If this is a trope, it's in the 1-bundle that helps to constitute Jo. (For simplicity I leave world indices aside.) But if 'that Jo is a good girl' is to be analyzed along the lines of §§7A9, 7B9, then Jo's 1-bundle must already be available before the proposition that Jo is a good girl is determined. Yet this proposition is already needed for J's believing trope to go into her 1-bundle. Circularity threatens.

7C8   Infinite regress?

The fact that believings can embed simple propositions corresponding to tropes gives rise to another kind of circularity or recursion. If p is such a proposition, and believings are tropes, then we shall get infinitely many tropes

>   Jo's believing that p
>   Jo's believing that she believes that p
>   Jo's believing that she believes that she believes that p
>   ⋮

per believer (some of them nonexistent). Indeed, at every order of nesting, all tropes of the next lower order will be embedded (including those of other believers). While it is quite on the cards that there will be this many compound states of affairs (through iteration of connectives, etc.), it strains credulity to admit so many "simple" states of affairs or tropes.

7C9   Irreducible relation?

A reasonable conclusion might be that believings are not tropes but complexes of a distinctive kind. We have already recognized elements in our trope theory that are not tropes, such as the metarelations of concurrence, likeness, and precedence. Even if these can be reduced to bundles of higher-level tropes, some metarelations will remain at the higher level (§§1B5, 5A9). Unlike Campbell (1990: ch. 1), I don't claim a one-category ontology. Perhaps, then, we must simply recognize belief, or doxastic accessibility, as one more irreducible relation needed for a trope theory of the mind.

Yet I can't quite shake the picture of Jo's beliefs as part of Jo, of the belief relation as the bundle of all believings. It's not to be ruled out that believings are tropes of some sort. If they are, I haven't yet seen where to accommodate them in the theory.[10]

7C10   Taking stock

I've provided a structural metaphysical framework for belief that solves some puzzles and clarifies some problems. The approach will likely be felt to be idiosyncratic. All the same, I hope some will also find it suggestive or provocative. While it doesn't depend on trope theory, I was led to it by a consideration of state-of-affairs concepts (propositions) as a generalization of trope-concepts. And the use of tropes softens the ontological pinch of possible worlds. Needless to say, much more remains to be said about belief – conceptually by epistemologists, theoretically by cognitive scientists, empirically by psychologists. Belief is a genuinely interdisciplinary concern.[11]

8

Furthering the Cause

8A Causation Defined

8A1 Pervasiveness of causation

For a concept so absolutely central to our thinking about the world and our understanding of it, efficient causation has proved surprisingly recalcitrant to precise analysis. Aristotle compared it to his three other kinds of "cause". Kant made it his most popular "category", or pure concept of the understanding.[1] Causation has traditionally been considered central to natural science, although this has been disputed for twentieth-century physics.[2] It appears to be presupposed by a good part of our body of law, civil and criminal. The influential moral philosophy of utilitarianism assumes causation in tracing out the consequences of actions to rate them as right or wrong. Action theory is obliged to supplement proximate agent causation by efficient causation in order to comprehend what an agent brings about. What, then, is this causal relation, and what does it relate?

8A2 Causal relata

What sort of things are causes and effects? Leaving aside causal agents (e.g. God) and objectual causes (billiard balls),[3] the standard candidates are events, i.e., by my lights, tropes of a particularly lively sort (§1A3 above). Since, however, a complex cause may involve more than one trope, the general case calls for our states of affairs, which can do duty as compound tropes (§§3D4ff). While other theories of states of affairs might do as well for this purpose, it seems particularly natural to start with tropes as the basic causes and effects.

8A3   Hyperintensionality?

As what are usually called propositions, our states of affairs would seem to make causal contexts intensional. The question arises whether they are not in fact, like belief contexts, *hyper*intensional, as some have urged. We recall that logical equivalence is a sufficient condition for state-of-affairs identity. Could we have

$p \dashv\vdash q$
p causes r
q doesn't cause r?

I think not; perhaps the worst case would be something like

$p \dashv\vdash p \mathrel{\&} (q \lor \sim q)$
p causes r
$\therefore p \mathrel{\&} (q \lor \sim q)$ causes r.

But I think we might bite the bullet here and argue that p and $p \mathrel{\&} (q \lor \sim q)$ are the same state of affairs and, if p is an event, the same event. If so, how could they differ in their effects? Accordingly, it seems appropriate to take causation as intensional but not hyperintensional, and its relata as states of affairs, not propositions (state-of-affairs concepts). In this I follow Lewis (1973b) (terminology appropriately adjusted).

8A4   Kinds of cause

Even if we confine our attention to efficient causation, we find a battery of closely related concepts in use (see figure 8.1). In analogy to logical conditionals, we might expect that the conjunction of all the necessary causes of a given event would yield its

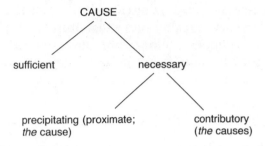

Figure 8.1

sufficient cause. Although this is not perhaps absolutely obvious, it would seem to be guaranteed by the "law of causality" (the principle of sufficient ground). Often we're inclined to take the precipitating cause of an event to be its latest contributory cause. Which contributory cause is latest is, of course, a contingent matter, and in any case it's often an earlier cause that precipitates. Thus the precipitating cause is relative to contingent circumstances obtaining in the particular possible world concerned, including perhaps our own interests. For 'precipitating cause' we frequently say '*the* cause', for 'contributory causes' '*the* causes'. This brief discussion does not exhaust the ways we use '*the* cause'. For example, we now commonly accept that cigarette smoking is the cause of many cases of lung cancer; yet it is neither sufficient nor necessary nor precipitating; it is the "main" cause in some sense. All things considered, though, it appears that the basic notion is that of necessary cause, of a state of affairs *sine qua non*.

8A5   Overdetermination

A complication is created by the possibility of the causal over-determination of an event; for example, the death of Susan Caldwell owing to heart failure and her father's slap at the same time in Trilling's (1957: 289).[4] The blow and the heart failure each appear to be "contributory", yet one would have been enough, making neither "necessary". What shall we say? I say that the *disjunction* was the cause. I know there is a lot of resistance to allowing disjunctions to do anything. It is felt that disjunctive states of affairs don't really exist, that it is always one of the disjuncts that operates. But when we can never tell which, how warranted are we in holding out for a determinate disjunct *in re*? Logically, the disjunction is the obvious solution.

8A6   *Veridicity*

We call seeing veridical when it "gets its man", when "seeing that" is factive, when what we seem to see is really there. Similarly,

> $p, \therefore q$
> From p I infer that q[5]
> q because p
> p caused q

are all factive, entailing p and q. We might call the last the *thick* sense of 'cause', expressing "veridical" causation. The thick sense can also be expressed as 'actually cause'. In the logic of perception, there is much to be said for taking nonveridical seeing as primitive (cf. Bacon 1979: 273ff). I propose to take an analogous *thin* sense of 'cause' as basic. (Nothing much hangs on this decision: the converse definition appears equally workable.) In the thin sense 'p caused q' implies neither p nor q; it means rather that if p occurred, it would have caused q. The more colloquial thick sense is then definable:

> p veridically causes $q =_{df} p$ & (p causes q) & q

For this slightly technical thin sense of 'causes' I introduce the symbol '–c'.

8A7   *Laws and subjunctives*

It seems clear that

> $(p -c\ q) \rightarrow (\sim p\ \square\rightarrow \sim q)$:

a necessary causal condition (p) is a necessary condition (in something like the Lewis–Stalnaker sense of a subjunctive conditional), but not always vice versa: a necessary condition need not be causal. What more is needed than a necessary condition for a cause? Causation seems to have something to do with the laws of nature L. Perhaps we should say something like

$$(p -\!\text{c}\ q) \to (L\ \&\ \sim p \ \square\!\!\to\ \sim q)$$

or

$$(p -\!\text{c}\ q) \to [L \ \|\!\!= (\sim p \ \square\!\!\to\ \sim q)].$$

(For "$\|\!\!=$" see §7B5.) The former is too weak: a world like ours except that $\sim p$ will have the same laws L as ours, making 'L' superfluous. The latter, however, looks promising.

8A8   Relevance

In view of the paradox of subjunctive implication,

$$\vdash\ \sim p\ \&\ \sim q \to (\sim p \ \square\!\!\to\ \sim q),$$

and other questionable theses of the Lewis–Stalnaker logic of counterfactuals, some connection of relevance seems to be called for. Ultimately the relevance connection ought to be built into the conditional $\square\!\!\to$. I omit the details here; what I have in mind would be something like this:

$$(p \ \square\!\!\to\ q)_\alpha =_{\text{df}} \forall w[(p_w\ \&\ w \text{ is sufficiently like } \alpha) \text{ relevantly}$$
implies q_w].

By "relevantly implies" here is meant something like Anderson and Belnap's relevant implication (1975: §§3, 28).[6] For details of such a relevant subjunctive conditional, see Routley (1989: 294–7).

8A9 *Time order*

It remains to build in the "arrow" or directionality of causation. Classically this is a matter of temporal precedence; latterly subtler, partly subjectivist accounts have been forthcoming (see Menzies and Price 1993). Having nothing to contribute to the latter, I will stick with temporal precedence $<$ as a placeholder for a more adequate account:

$$p -\!c\ q =_{\text{df}} (p < q)\ \&\ [L \parallel= (\sim p\ \Box\!\!\rightarrow \sim q)].$$

It might ultimately turn out that $<$ can be fruitfully be replaced by $\leq$. (In §6A5, $<$ was introduced as a relation of tropes; in §6A9 it was extended to states of affairs.)

8A10 *Sufficient cause*

The sufficient cause (in the thin sense) of a state of affairs is, as we observed in §8A4, the conjunction of all its necessary causal conditions:

$$p\ \mathbf{C}\ q =_{\text{df}} p \dashv\!\vdash \bigvee_r (r -\!c\ q)$$

Notice that in the case of alternative contributory causes, this definition wouldn't work without the disjunctions embraced in §8A5. A thick (and more normal) sense of sufficient cause can now be defined as in §8A6:

$$p \text{ is all it takes for } q =_{\text{df}} p\ \&\ (p\ \mathbf{C}\ q)\ \&\ q$$

With that we have defined thick and thin senses of necessary causation and sufficient causation as relations of states of affairs. In the case of simple states of affairs, corresponding to tropes, causal relations of tropes are induced. Once again, tropes prove useful (though not indispensable) for clarifying a difficult (meta)-physical concept.

9

Duty and Better Worlds

9A Obligation Defined

9A1 Inherent goodness

While I personally have long preferred a deontological approach to
ethical theory, Campbell has pointed out that "On a trope analysis,
the immediate object of evaluation is the trope" (1981: 481). The
suggestion has sufficient prima facie plausibility that it is worth
exploring. 'Good' is a qualifying adjective; like a monadic adverb
it stands for a property, a set of tropes (cf. §3A9): tropes of being
good so-and-so's, of doing such-and-such well. Now, some goods
are nonmoral: good plagiarists, good hit men, good brooms. I
leave these aside. I am interested only in goods that enhance the
world: good men, good will, good actions. I will call these
"inherently good".[1]

9A2 Betterness and quality of tropes

"Good" or "inherently good" will not be our basic axiological
concept, however, but rather "better". "Inherently better than" is
a dyadic adverb or qualifying adjective (see §3B4). As such
it stands for a dyadic metarelation (set of trope pairs). This
metarelation is irreflexive, asymmetric, and transitive, like
temporal precedence. As tropes are the subjects of goodness, so
they are the field of betterness. This field T is to betterness as a

single time line is to precedence (§6A6). Substituting T for such a time line and betterness for precedence, we can now recapitulate the development of §§6A7ff, with the simplification that a trope does not occupy a range of goodness (like the time of a trope) but a single determinate point. Call this analogue of a time point the *quality* $Q(t)$ of the trope t. Since the quality (like the time point) is a trope, it will belong to the field of betterness.

9A3   Improving worlds

Given a possible world, it might at first seem like a good idea to replace one of its tropes by an inherently better one. Yet, as Descartes warned, the whole may be the better for an imperfect part (1641: ch. 4, part 6). Improving one trope is not guaranteed to improve the world. In any case, replacing one trope may have far-reaching repercussions. Perhaps we may take a leaf here from the theory of belief revision as developed by philosopher-logicians (Alchourrón, Gärdenfors, & Makinson 1985; Gärdenfors 1988) and vigorously investigated by computer scientists.[2] The theory seeks the most rational way of revising one's beliefs in the face of a new piece of information. Analogously, we can ask how the world (a set of tropes) must be revised to accommodate one trope replacement. (We include addition and deletion, i.e. replacement of an absent trope and replacement by an already present one.) Assume that belief-revision theory, together with causal considerations, yields an answer. Then check to see whether the resulting adjustment has somehow made things worse. For example, it may be that as trope t was replaced by its improvement t', another trope s had to give way to its inferior s'. If

$$Q(t') - Q(t) \geq Q(s) - Q(s'),$$

then the change can be sustained as an improvement, or at any rate as harmless. In an actual case, of course, the comparisons would be much more complicated. Thus (very roughly) world improvement is characterized in terms of trope improvement.

9A4 Better worlds: duty

Given an account of what it is to improve a world by replacing tropes ("v is an improvement on w"), the ancestral of the improvement relation will be a relation of inherent betterness of worlds: "v is better than w", "w is worse than v", in short $w\Sigma v$.[3] We can now plug Σ into the standard truth condition for obligation in deontic logic:

$$|OA|_w = T \text{ iff } \forall v(w\Sigma v \rightarrow |A|_v = T)$$
$$\text{i.e. } \overleftarrow{\Sigma}{}'w \subseteq |A|.$$

With that, we have defined 'ought' in terms of 'good', the central axiological project. And though we have ranked qualities of tropes, we have come up with a basis for axiology that is not, as one might have expected, explicitly consequentialist or utilitarian.

9A5 Axiology triumphant?

Just as defining disjunction in terms of conjunction and negation doesn't show that conjunction has any primacy over disjunction, so our definition of 'ought' doesn't necessarily show that it is secondary to 'good'. Conceivably the converse order of definition might work. In any case, the core insight of deontology is that ethics is about regulating actions, conduct, and attitudes, not about multiplying cold gems of intrinsic value. That stands no matter what the order of definition. All the same, the possibility of an axiological definition is instructive. It means that we need not take deontic accessibility (Σ) as primitive, but only the metarelation of inherent betterness of tropes. Thus a plausible approach to ethical theory is not only integrated into trope theory, but finds a clarifying basis in trope theory.

9B   Conclusion

9B1   A case for tropes

While it is undoubtedly fruitful to continue exploring and comparing other approaches, trope theory emerges favorably from the above metaphysical applications. Time, cause, belief, and duty work relatively smoothly in this framework. It seems to offer the right balance of ontological economies and architectonic opportunities. Finally, recall the epistemological point made at the outset (§§1A1, 1A4): tropes are what we're acquainted with first of all. Without embracing phenomenalism, we can appreciate the virtue of founding our metaphysic on the sort of things we directly know. In the end, the way of being and the way of knowing crisscross and shore each other up. It would be heartening if they led to nothing stranger than tropes.

Notes

1 TROPES, UNIVERSALS, AND INDIVIDUALS

1 In Greek 'trope' means "turn"; in rhetoric, "turn of phrase" or "figure of speech". According to Williams, Santayana used it for 'essence of an occurrence'. Considering these senses of the word virtually useless, Williams appropriated it for 'occurrence of an essence' (1953: 78). By now we are pretty much stuck with his *jeu de mot*. The idea of tropes goes back at least to G. F. Stout (1971a), who called them "characters" or "abstract particulars" (1971b: 1178). The best candidate, in my opinion, to replace Williams's buzz word, is Levinson's "quality-bit" (1980: 108) and, analogously, "relation-bit". In place of "-bit", "token" would not be inappropriate. One might also consider using Peirce's prefix "sin-", as in "sinsign" (1931–58: 2.245).

2 This conception is essentially due to Cresswell (developing a thread of Wittgenstein (1922), of course): "We are to suppose that we are given a set **B** of 'basic particular situations'. The idea is that any subset w of **B** determines a possible world" (1973: 38). Cf. also Armstrong: "The simplest way to specify a possible world would be to say that *any conjunction* of possible atomic states of affairs . . . constitutes such a world" (1989a: 47).

3 Campbell often uses 'fact' in this way, e.g. 1990: 100.

4 Pettit made this point in a discussion of an earlier version of chapter 2 read at the Australian National University on May 8, 1987.

5 Cf. David Lewis on the nonrigidity of event description (1973b: 562 n. 9).

6 I am indebted to Sally Palmer for clarifying the role of transferability for me in this debate (1989).

7 Since for Armstrong the conjunction of two coinstantiated universals is a universal (1978b: 30ff), if he were to admit *particularized* universals, i.e. tropes, then presumably he would admit conjunctive ones too. And his "thick" particulars are conjunctive states of affairs. Thus he comes close to compound tropes.

8   Michael Devitt made this point to me in the discussion of an earlier version of my 1988 essay read in Sydney on September 16, 1985.

9   Actualism is supported by Quine's criterion of ontological commitment (1953a), of which I have felt the force (1987a). Here, however, I take the direction of free logic, which permits us to refer to and, by extension, to quantify over nonexistents. I concede the peculiarity of putting nonexistents to work in one's theory. The sense of that peculiarity is the root intuition of actualism. But the adequate theory may turn out to be peculiar.

10 Confusion is unlikely with the (astro)physical meaning, namely, a mass of gas (usually rotating) whose equation of state describes an Emden function.

11 In recognizing simple first-level relational tropes, I part company with Campbell, who reconstrues them as second-level tropes relating first-level tropes (§2A2 below). With Armstrong (1989b: 126), I consider it desirable to maintain a parallelism between properties and relations, monadic and polyadic tropes.

12 Hochberg makes heavy weather of this in his critique of trope theory (1988: 203–6), as does Campbell in answering him (1990: 62–5). I fail to see what the fuss is all about.

13 Levels (in contradistinction to types) are defined as follows. (Concrete) particulars (individuals, items of type 0) are considered to be (degenerate) tropes of level 0. Relations among tropes of level i are relations of level i. Tropes of relations of level i are tropes of level $i + 1$. Level 0 is also called ground-level. Thus my use of 'level' differs somewhat from Campbell's, as well as from Campbell and Armstrong's use of 'order'. Little hangs on the departure. The motivation for my usage is to be found in Bacon 1989.

14 But cf. §1A5: the common subject is the grammatical expression of concurrence, not necessarily the indication of an ingredient individual.

15 Actually, my view is that mathematics and set theory are one, of which logic is part. But I don't prejudge the question whether set theory might ultimately be based on category theory or mereology. (Interestingly, in the seventeenth century mathematics was sometimes equated with metaphysics.) What I put forward here is my picture of the disciplinary relationships. If the reader prefers a different picture, it may be that not too much hangs on the disagreement. My main aim is to secure the availability of set theory as a tool, against those who find it metaphysically problematic.

16 The actual world is a set of existent tropes. A proper subset of it would be inactual, even though all its members existed. There is no simple law relating the existence of a set to that of its members. On the propriety of referring to nonexistents, cf. n. 9 above.

17 It may be that the structure of physical objects is captured best in mereology, the theory of wholes and their parts. Mereology, in turn, can be embedded in set theory. On the other hand, David Lewis has suggested the converse reduction (1986), in which case mereology would subsume the general theory of structure.

18 In my view, this is the only version of trope theory worth pursuing. Martin

(1980) and Armstrong (1989b: 114, 116, 127) prefer a "substance–attribute" version that I find needlessly complicated. Küng finds it already in Aristotelian–Thomistic philosophy (1963: 141). Cf. §§1A8, 5C3.

19   Carnap's *Ähnlichkeiten* (1929: 48); bundles he called *Ähnlichkeitskreise* (1929: §20b).

20   If $X \subset Y$, then in Carnap's terms Y is a *"companion"* of X (1928: §70). Companionship is thus prohibited to bundles. If the items to be represented by the bundles nevertheless require companionship, we have the "companionship problem". Cf. §1D5 below.

21   Thus the "tightness", like the equivalence, is relative to a specification of the equivalence relation involved.

22   In previous writings, I tried 'persimilitude', 'consortium' (1988: 96), and 'correlation' (1988: 107). The trouble with 'precise similarity' is that it suggests transitivity and it suggests that similar individuals are involved.

23   If the given trope is what I have called elsewhere a "kernel" (1989: §10), then actual transitivity as such is not required by Williams here. A *kernel* is a trope such that any tropes like it are like each other. I leave it open whether universals have kernels. These might be helpful for dealing with Goodman's problem of imperfect community (1951: 125); cf. my 1989 n. 6.

24   For the sake of the example, it is assumed that likeness of color tropes involves sharing a color. If the example wants plausibility, narrow the color range.

25   Peter Forrest has made this point (1993: §1.3).

26   It might be objected that there is more to an individual than a bundle, that the concurring of the member tropes ought to be right in there as a kind of glue. Perhaps some such consideration motivated Williams's fusion. The glue would serve no purpose, however; it is enough that the bundle is an equivalence class under the equivalence relation of concurrence.

27   Sally Palmer (1989: 4) has made it clear to me that variability or externality of concurrence is tantamount to what Armstrong calls transferability (1989b: 117f), allowing that a trope might be removed from an individual's bundle or swapped with another like trope. (If concurrence is accidental, then Socrates' whiteness might just as well have been Plato's, and vice versa.)

28   Some primitive predication is indispensable, e.g. statements of set-membership.

2   RELATIONAL TROPES AND INDIVIDUALS

1   In Armstrong's terms (1989a: 103), this would mean that substances or monadic qualities supervene on relations! (Armstrong uses 'supervene' differently from Campbell.)

2   Notice that, since A uniquely characterizes a, extensionally it is the singleton $\{a\}$. Thus $A \times B = \{a\} \times \{b\} = \{\langle a, b \rangle\}$.

3   The ambiguity in our use of 'relation' of course extends to the way the terms

are related. A relation *qua* bundle overlaps its terms. A relating or trope is a member of its terms. A set-theoretic relation has n-tuples of terms as members.

4   As the order is already given by the indices of the i-concurrence relations employed, the unordered set $\{a^1,\ a^2,\dots\}$ would do as well, as Keith Campbell has pointed out to me. For the sake of clarity I will continue to write it as a sequence.

5   I.e., the relation whose extension is $\{x_1,\dots,x_n\colon x_1 = x_1 \&\dots\& x_n = x_n\}$.

6   "§" is Kneale's symbol for "that" (1962: 539), like "-ing" a nominalizing affix.

7   This construction is exploited below in connection with the substance-attribute version of trope theory, which eschews bundling (§5C7).

3   COMPOUND UNIVERSALS, WHOLES, AND STATES OF AFFAIRS

1   The above construction of compound properties exactly parallels Stelzner's construction of the "relevant fulfilment conditions" in his semantics of relevant deontic logic (1992: 197). I adapted the construction from van Fraassen (1975: 227).

2   The example relies on our recognition that cordateness is a different property from renateness, since hearts are not kidneys. On the intuitive individuation of tropes by properties, see §1A4.

3   The treatment of adverbs sketched here does not extend to gerund phrases sometimes used to refer to tropes. "Slowly" or "slowness" modifies properties, not tropes.

4   By 'particularism' I mean what Armstrong calls "class nominalism", misleadingly, I believe (1978a: 28ff.). The insistence that the classes or functions used in model theory to interpret predicates are not universals, even when quantified over, makes "nominalism" too easy.

5   According to Armstrong's definition (1978b), it appears that a structural property must involve at least one nonmereological relation. It is a natural generalization of his notion, however, to admit structural properties containing properties only, as a limiting case. Armstrong appears to make just this generalization (1989a: §5): "conjunctive universals . . . may be thought of as the simplest cases of structural universals."

6   Thus, according to Campbell, "There are complex derivative tropes" (1990: 20), but he doesn't tell us how they are formed. It's not clear that they are the same as his "quasi-tropes" or "derivative, local tropes" (1990: 152, 157) or his "conjunctive compresent complexes" (1990: 82) (which seem to be conjunctive properties). For that matter, Wittgenstein seems to have assumed that an account of truth-functions would make it clear how to get *Sachlagen* in general out of *Sachverhalte*.

7 I assume that T is a set, i.e. that all tropes can be members. But if T is a proper class, any subclass is a possible world, and any class of possible worlds is a state of affairs.

8 This construction seems to have originated with McKinsey (1949). It has been taken up by Schock (1962), van Fraassen (1975: 225), Skyrms (1989: 146), and Barwise and Perry (1983: 53). Van Fraassen calls such tuples "complexes", following Whitehead and Russell (1910–13: 44); Barwise and Perry call them "constituent sequences".

4 SEMANTICS, MODALITY, AND WORLD-LINES

1 It is easy to confuse models with possible worlds, as the two are indeed closely related historically and systematically. Just as necessity is truth in all worlds, so validity is truth in all models. But in modal contexts, each model typically contains a different set of possible worlds. If each model is stipulated to contain *all* possible worlds, we get Cocchiarella's "primary semantics of modality" (1975).

2 An interesting path not taken here confines the metarelations to the actual tropes in α, recombining the resulting individuals and universals to form the rest of the possible worlds (whether as fictions, *Ersätze*, or duly constituted alternatives). Thus, ignoring polyadic tropes for the moment, T becomes $H``\alpha \times I^{1``}\alpha$ (all likeness-bundle/1-concurrence-bundle pairs drawn from α). In the idiom of Barwise and Perry, α comprises the "real situations" and T the "abstract situations" (1983: 7ff). Although I do not know that such an approach has ever been shown to be semantically adequate, its actualism has undeniable appeal. Cf. Armstrong (1989a: 38–43).

3 In such systems, the phrase 'absolute domain' becomes ambiguous, depending upon whether it is the inner domains of existents in the respective worlds that are meant, or their comprehensive union with the outer domain (if any). I mean the latter.

4 For readers unfamiliar with these various modal systems, good introductions are Hughes and Cresswell (1968: 195–202) and Thomason's exposition of **Q2** in (1969: 131–7). The motivation of **Q4** is quite like that of **Q2**.

5 Straight world-lines are closely related to essentialism and "haecceitism". On one interpretation, a haecceity is just like a straight world-line except that it delivers, for a given world, the *singleton* of the world-line's value there.

6 Some examples: Quine's number-of-planets (n) argument (1953b: 143f):

$$\Box(9 > 7)$$
$$9 = n$$
$$\therefore \Box(n > 7)$$

This fails because, while '9' is a rigid designator, 'n' is not. The argument goes through if 'n' is replaced by the rigid designator '3^2'. For the next example, pretend that it is early 1985:

> Mike is engaged to Vanessa Williams.
> Mike is engaged to Miss America.
> Vanessa Williams is not necessarily identical to Miss America.
> ___
> ∴Mike is engaged to two women.

Here, 'Miss America' is a nonrigid designator of a crooked world-line, while the variable 'women' in the quantifier 'two women' ranges over straight world-lines only. The existential generalization is accordingly unwarranted. (Notice that although contingently Williams = Miss America, 'is not necessarily identical to' is an intensional predicate expressing diversity of world-lines:

$$\sim\Box(\text{Williams} = \text{Miss America}).)$$

7 Gupta gets impressive mileage out of construing common nouns as intensional predicates in this sense (1980). The intensional properties they express Gupta calls "sorts" (1980: 3).

8 Armstrong then introduces 'possible state of affairs' for what most people call "states of affairs" (1989a: 45); cf. Barwise and Perry's "abstract situations" (1983: 50).

9 The positions here are complicated by Armstrong's recognition of what he calls "non-Naturalist Actualism" (1989a: 31ff), e.g. R. M. Adams's use of propositions as a basis for modality 1974. For Armstrong himself, only the natural exists. If Adams's propositions are non-natural, then we could either take them as inactual or (with Armstrong and Adams himself) as actual but non-natural. It's a verbal dispute.

10 Another of those unpretty neologisms that litter the area, this one perpetrated by Lycan (1979: 305), Armstrong thinks (1989a: 46). It reminds one of the monster 'utilitarianism', which Windelband sensibly proposed to shorten to 'utilism' (1957: 439). So here we might say 'combinism' or, from the Romance, simply 'cambism'.

11 Cf. McX's dodge of identifying the nonexistent Pegasus with "an idea in men's minds" (1953a: 2).

12 Since I know that Armstrong would not accept this conclusion, what I believe he ought to do instead is to abandon interchangeability and therewith weak anti-haecceitism. This would in turn suggest a reconsideration of his doctrine of thick and thin particulars.

13 Modal pluralism was first suggested to me by Hanson (1963). The basic outlook was of course already implicit in von Wright (1951).

14 The need for such an analysis was suggested by Hanson, who called this

modality "technological possibility" (1963). A converse analysis of causation in terms of agent possibility has been put forward by my colleagues Menzies and Price (1993).

5 METARELATIONS AND METAPHYSICS

1   Hochberg has called the trope philosophy "moderate nominalism" (1988), and Skyrms finds a suggestion of "Tractarian nominalism" in Wittgenstein (1922). Simons advances a substance–attribute version of trope theory (1995; cf. §1A8) as the most viable form of "particularism" (1993). Armstrong once called trope theory "Particularism" (1978a: 78ff).

2   These relata may not exist; cf. ch. 1 n. 9; §§4B2, 1E8, 4C1. But the problem here is the status of the relations themselves rather than the relata.

3   Notice that such relations are not so heterogeneous, since world cores are sets of trope sets and individuals are sequences of sets of trope sets.

4   Actually, Campbell appears to take ϵ or at any rate ι (the singleton-forming function), as primitive (1990: 88). Presumably he would want to say that instances of the membership relation supervene upon their bases, and are therefore no ontological addition. But it is not clear that any such bases (property tropes) are available in Campbell's scheme, particularly when the terms of ϵ are other than individuals.

5   Kant allowed for the curious possibility of a divine understanding that would intuit directly without need of categories (1787: 145). It's hard for me to know what to make of that. It sounds like a counterexample to Kant's own claim. However, there is some indication that the divine being would not *think*, and hence would not be rational.

6   Remember that I use 'universals' for properties and relations in the wide sense, not just for undivided "ones" fully shared by many; cf. §1D10.

7   These are not the same as the states of affairs of part 3D.

8   This definition will not work when F or R^n is not syntropic. In that case F or R^n must be subdivided by adverbial modification into a set of syntropic subuniversals.

9   Of course this is not the usual sense of this term, but in this context a confusion with the American variant of Unitarianism is unlikely. The position is often called the "bundle theory". A version was advocated by Russell (1948: 312). It is reminiscent of Leibniz (1686), but he did not identify an individual substance (monad) with its complete concept, even though the two were intimately linked.

10 Armstrong calls particularism (in my sense, but without possible worlds) "class nominalism", for he holds that classes of particulars are particulars rather than universals (1978a: 15, 42), or "abstract entities", as Carnap, Quine, Sellars, and other American philosophers have called them. However, as particularism with possible worlds gives a tolerable (though ultimately

inadequate) account of properties and relations, it is misleading to call it a form of nominalism. (Armstrong has used 'Particularism' in another sense; cf. n. 1.)

6 TAKING TIME

1 Russell used events rather than tropes; the essential thing is that both occupy intervals. I owe the Russell reference to an anonymous referee.

2 Russell in effect assumes a single time line, as he is developing private time; cf. (1914: 96, I(d)).

3 The ancestral of $<>$ is the relation that holds between s and t when there are intermediate x_1, x_2, etc. such that $s <> x_1$, $x_1 <> x_2$, and so on up to $<> t$.

4 In constructing an instant, Russell says, "Let us take a group of events of which any two overlap, so that there is some time, however short, when they all exist" (1914: 95). When the construction is complete, that time will be the kernel.

5 Time intervals would be simpler if the time series were discrete, an empirical question according to Russell (1914: 96). Modern physics makes it dense and in fact continuous. (I am indebted to Graham Priest and Adrian Heathcote for clarification of this point.)

6 Cf. Russell's definition of "duration" (1936: 350). If t has temporal gaps, like the Hundred Years' War or my writing this book or John o' Gaunt's affaire with Katherine Swinford, then $\mathfrak{T}(t)$ would not be an interval. But if that case it would be natural to assume that we were dealing with two or more tropes. I leave this complication aside for now; cf.§6B3 below.

7 In keeping with §3A5, '$t \in$' would read '$\{t\}\in$'. That complication is beside the point here. k_w is the core of w, its tropes (§4B5).

8 In the story, Brigadoon has its own time line: the inhabitants are not aware of gaps. Ignore this detail. If Brigadoon is too complex to be an individual, take instead a pebble in Brigadoon.

9 I owe this example to Graham Priest.

10 Notation: '+' for mereological sum or fusion; '¶' for 'is part of'. For '§' see §4A6.

11 For if a has an essence in the sense of §6B2, it follows that $\exists i \, \forall w \in W(E_w a \to t \in a^i_w)$ and, by existential generalization, $\exists i \, \exists t \in T \, \exists w \in W(E_w a \to t \in a^i_w)$. The latter makes a straight in the sense of §4A7, but with the existence condition added. Thus 'a' is rigid, subject to the existence condition.

12 *Pace* Aristotle, according to whom a dead man can become unhappy if his descendants turn out badly (1925: 1100ª20). Similarly, posthumous canonization cannot change a mortal, I hold.

13 This term is appropriated from Wollheim (1984), who introduced it in a rather different sense. My use is a special case of Campbell's, for whom a thread is any temporal trope other than a kernel (1981: 487).

7   BELIEF

1   The vivid barbarism loses something when replaced by the etymologically correct 'creditum'.

2   An *X*-concept is for Church a sense determining an *X* (1978: 168). In the possible-world reconstruction of Fregean semantics, an *X*-concept is a function from possible worlds to *X*s.

3   Although trope theory is not essential to this account of belief, it grew out of the idea of taking believees to be functions from worlds to tropes or, more generally, states of affairs. Notice that, unlike Frege and Church, I take a state of affairs (not a truth-value) to be the referent of a declarative sentence or a 'that'-clause. Barwise and Perry have made a similar move, with situations in place of states of affairs (1983: 21–4). Similarly, I take properties to be the referents (not the senses) of one-place predicates (cf. §7A7).

4   If possible worlds are sets of tropes, then a single trope t will yield two worlds Λ, $\{t\}$ and four states of affairs Λ, $\{\Lambda\}$, $\{\{t\}\}$, $\{\Lambda, \{t\}\}$. Thus there will be 16 functions from worlds to states of affairs. And since Λ and $\{t\}$ each support just one concurrence relation, it and the more complicated worlds of §4B5 can be ignored in this count.

5   Propositions as dyadic relations have already been studied in so-called "two-dimensional modal logic" (e.g. Segerberg 1973). The idea is also broached in effect by David Lewis with his "three-place truth relation: truth *of* a sentence φ *at* a world *i* *with reference to* a world *j*" (1973a: 62). Lewis's connective † is an object-language counterpart of my $=$ functor, which was introduced in Bacon (1987: 148) as an alternative notation for Quine's predicate functor 'T'. Propositions were introduced by Stalnaker (1978) under the name 'propositional concepts'.

6   This may not be familiar as a logical equivalence, but it is so in predicate-functor logic with proper names.

7   Intuitions about such examples diverge to some extent. There are those who consider some logical equivalences so crashingly obvious that no one could possibly believe the one equivalent without the other. Yet this seems to be an empirical claim: the impossibility is psychological, not logical. It may help to think in terms of a less obvious example. I chose the passivization equivalence mainly for its brevity.

8   This admittedly leaves open the question what it is to understand '&', if not to believe in accordance with conjunction introduction, elimination, etc. One can understand 'Cicero' without knowing its entire encyclopedia entry (complete with gentile name). Presumably one can understand '&' without knowing the relevant chapter of a logic textbook.

9   If we develop '$\Vdash$' as a propositional predicate and relativize its truth conditions suitably to worlds, then we get the full calculus of pure strict **S5** implication.

10 It would, of course, be open to us to particularize the irreducible relation

into tropes without expecting to get the terms out by concurrence bundling. This would amount to taking Martin's substance–attribute approach (1980) or Campbell's foundationist approach (1990: 101) to believing (or to all propositional attitudes) alone. But I consider these to be less satisfactory versions of trope theory (cf. §§1A7, 2A2).

11 It is the concern of belief theory or "doxology", as it might appropriately be called. In the philosophical youth culture of the 1980s it sometimes went by the "sexy" name of 'cognitive science' (the "cognition" in question being not knowledge in the first instance but belief).

8 FURTHERING THE CAUSE

1 Of Kant's twelve categories, the one almost always cited as an example is causality; occasionally substance is mentioned. (When did you last hear of an application of the category of reciprocal operation of agent and patient?)

Note that 'causality' has more or less given way to 'causation' in recent parlance. From the Latin, this convenient barbarism would mean "giving as a reason or pretext", not "causing".

2 Cf. Russell: "the reason why physics has ceased to look for causes is that, in fact, there are no such things. The law of causality, I believe, . . . is a relic of a bygone age, surviving, like the monarchy, only because it is erroneously supposed to do no harm" (1912: 174).

3 Note that French 'chose' ("thing") comes from Latin 'causa'.

4 In the story, the blow causes the heart attack, but Duck's ignorance of his daughter's heart condition is extenuating. My example takes liberties with the plot.

5 'Infer' is not always factive in the nonperformative second and third persons, nor in the past; e.g., 'From his clothing I inferred that he was a woman.'

6 Relevance logic has by now flowered so richly, not to say rankly, that it is hard to keep up with "the one true logic". For an interesting recent departure in this direction, see the work of Brady, e.g. 1992.

9 DUTY AND BETTER WORLDS

1 One could also say 'intrinsically good', but that suggests 'essentially good' and thus 'necessarily good', as well as Moore's use of the phrase (1912: 37, 101).

2 I have in mind particularly the work of Sydney's Knowledge Study Group, led by Norman Foo and his colleagues.

3 Think of 'Σ' as a 'W' (for 'worse') on its side, or as a double '$<$'.

References

Adams, Robert N. 1974: "Theories of actuality", *Noûs* 8: 211–31. Reprinted in Loux 1979: 190–209.

Alchourrón, Carlos E., Gärdenfors, Peter, and Makinson, David 1985: "On the logic of theory change: partial meet functions for contraction and revision", *Journal of Symbolic Logic* 50: 510–30.

Anderson, Alan Ross 1958: "A reduction of deontic logic to alethic modal logic", *Mind* 67: 100–3.

Anderson, Alan Ross 1966: "The formal analysis of normative systems", in *The Logic of Decision and Action*, ed. Nicholas Rescher, Pittsburgh: University of Pittsburgh Press, 147–213.

Anderson, Alan Ross and Belnap, Nuel D., Jr. 1975: *Entailment: The Logic of Relevance and Necessity*, vol. 1, Princeton: Princeton University Press.

Aristotle 1925: *Ethica Nicomachea*, tr. and ed. W. D. Ross, in *Works* vol. 9, Oxford: Clarendon Press.

Armstrong, D. M. 1978a: *Nominalism and Realism*, vol. 1 of *Universals and Scientific Realism*, Cambridge: Cambridge University Press.

Armstrong, D. M. 1978b: *A Theory of Universals*, vol. 2 of *Universals and Scientific Realism*, Cambridge: Cambridge University Press.

Armstrong, D. M. 1989a: *A Combinatorial Theory of Possibility*, Cambridge: Cambridge University Press.

Armstrong, D. M. 1989b: *Universals: An Opinionated Introduction*, Boulder CO: Westview Press.

Bacon, John 1966: *Being and Existence: Two Ways of Formal Ontology*, dissertation, Yale University.

Bacon, John 1971: "The generic conception of the universal", *Scientific Report* 10, Applied Logic Branch, Hebrew University of Jerusalem, March.

Bacon, John 1973: "Do generic descriptions denote?", *Mind* 82: 331–47.

Bacon, John 1974: "The untenability of genera", *Logique et analyse* 17: 197–208.

Bacon, John 1975a: "Belief as relative knowledge", in *The Logical Enterprise*

(Fitch Festschrift), ed. A. R. Anderson, R. B. Marcus, and R. M. Martin, New Haven: Yale University Press, 189–210.

Bacon, John 1975b: *Basic Logic, Extensional and Modal* (duplicated), New York: York College; 17th printing University of Sydney, 1993.

Bacon, John 1979: "The logical form of perception sentences", *Synthese* 41: 271–308.

Bacon, John 1980a: "Substance and first-order quantification over individual-concepts", *Journal of Symbolic Logic* 45: 193–203.

Bacon, John 1980b: "What is physical necessity?" *Proceedings of the Russellian Society* 5 (Sydney): 12–26.

Bacon, John 1985: "The completeness of a predicate-functor logic", *Journal of Symbolic Logic* 50: 903–26.

Bacon, John 1986: "Armstrong's theory of properties", *Australasian Journal of Philosophy* 64: 47–53.

Bacon, John 1987a: "A model-theoretic criterion of ontology", *Synthese* 72: 1–18.

Bacon, John 1987b: "Sommers and modern logic", in *The New Syllogistic*, ed. George Englebretsen, New York and Berne: Peter Lang, 121–60.

Bacon, John 1988: "Four modal modelings", *Journal of Philosophical Logic* 17: 91–114.

Bacon, John 1989: "A single primitive trope relation", *Journal of Philosophical Logic* 18: 141–54.

Bacon, John (forthcoming): "Weak supervenience supervenes", *Supervenience: New Essays*, eds E. E. Savellos and Ü. D. Yalçin, Cambridge: Cambridge University Press.

Bacon, John (unpublished): "Generic terms".

Barwise, Jon and Perry, John 1983: *Situations and Attitudes*, Cambridge MA: MIT-Bradford.

Brady, Ross T. 1992: "Hierarchical semantics for relevant logics", *Journal of Philosophical Logic* 21: 357–74.

Bressan, Aldo 1972: *A General Interpreted Modal Calculus*, New Haven: Yale University Press.

Burks, Arthur W. 1951: "The logic of causal propositions", *Mind* 60: 363–82.

Campbell, Keith 1981: "The metaphysic of abstract particulars", *Midwest Studies in Philosophy* 6: 477–88.

Campbell, Keith 1990: *Abstract Particulars*, Oxford: Blackwell.

Carnap, Rudolf 1928: *Der logische Aufbau der Welt*, Berlin: Weltkreis-Verlag; 3rd edn Hamburg: Meiner, 1966.

Carnap, Rudolf 1929: *Abriss der Logistik mit besonderer Berücksichtigung der Relationstheorie und ihrer Anwendungen*, Vienna: Springer.

Carnap, Rudolf 1947: *Meaning and Necessity: A Study in Semantics and Modal Logic*, Chicago: University of Chicago Press; enlarged 1956.

Church, Alonzo 1951: "The weak theory of implication", in *Kontrolliertes Denken: Untersuchungen zum Logikkalkül und der Logik der Einzelwissenschaften* (Festschrift Britzlmayr), ed. Albert Menne et al., Munich: Karl Alber, 22–37.

Church, Alonzo 1978: "The need for abstract entities in semantic analysis", in *Contemporary Philosophical Logic*, ed. I. M. Copi and J. A. Gould, New York: St Martin's, 166–76.

Cocchiarella, Nino B. 1975: "On the primary and secondary semantics of logical necessity", *Journal of Philosophical Logic* 4: 13–27.

Cotton, J. Harry 1951: *Christian Knowledge of God*, New York: Macmillan.

Cresswell, M. J. 1972: "Intensional logics and logical truth", *Journal of Philosophical Logic* 1: 2–15.

Cresswell, M. J. 1973: *Logics and Languages*, London: Methuen.

Cresswell, M. J. 1975: "Hyperintensional logic", *Studia Logica* 34: 25–38.

Cresswell, M. J. 1979: "The world is everything that is the case", in Loux 1979: 129–45.

Descartes, René 1641: *Meditationes de prima philosophia*, tr. Duc de Luynes, in *Oeuvres*, eds Adam and Tannery, Paris: Ministère de l'Instruction Publique, 1897–1913.

Devitt, Michael 1984: *Realism and Truth*, Oxford: Blackwell.

Fitch, Frederic B. 1952: *Symbolic Logic: An Introduction*, New York: Ronald.

Forrest, Peter 1993: "Just like quarks? The status of repeatables", in *Ontology, Causality and Mind: Essays in Honour of D. M Armstrong*, eds J. Bacon, K. Campbell, and L. Reinhardt, Cambridge: Cambridge University Press, 45–65.

Fraassen, Bas C. van 1975: "Facts and tautological entailments", in Anderson and Belnap 1975: 221–30.

Frege, Gottlob 1879: *Begriffsschrift: eine der arithmetischen nachgebildete Formelsprache des reinen Denkens*, Halle: Louis Nebert.

Frege, Gottlob 1892: "Über Sinn und Bedeutung", *Zeitschrift für Philosophie und philosophische Kritik* 100: 25–50.

Gärdenfors, Peter 1988: *Knowledge in Flux: Modeling the Dynamics of Epistemic States*, Cambridge MA: MIT-Bradford.

Goodman, Nelson 1951: *The Structure of Appearance*, Cambridge MA: Harvard University Press.

Gupta, Anil 1980: *The Logic of Common Nouns: An Investigation in Quantified Modal Logic*, New Haven: Yale University Press.

Hanson, Norwood Russell 1963: "The modalities in physical theory", class, Yale University, New Haven.

Heinlein, Robert A. 1953: "Jerry was a man", *Assignment in Eternity*, Reading, Pa.: Fantasy Press, 229–56.

Hintikka, Jaakko 1962: *Knowledge and Belief: An Introduction to the Logic of the Two Notions*, Ithaca: Cornell University Press.

Hochberg, Herbert 1988: "A refutation of moderate nominalism", *Australasian Journal of Philosophy* 66: 188–207.

Hughes, G. E. and Cresswell, M. J. 1968: *An Introduction to Modal Logic*, London: Methuen.

Jespersen, Otto 1924: *Philosophy of Grammar*, London: Allen and Unwin.

Kanger, Stig 1957: "The Morning Star paradox", *Theoria* 23: 1–11.

Kant, Immanuel 1781: *Kritik der reinen Vernunft*, 1st edn, Riga: Johann Friedrich Hartknoch.

Kant, Immanuel 1787: *Kritik der reinen Vernunft*, 2nd edn, Riga: Johann Friedrich Hartknoch.

Kneale, William and Kneale, Martha 1962: *The Development of Logic*, Oxford: Clarendon Press.

Kripke, Saul A. 1959: "A completeness theorem in modal logic", *Journal of Symbolic Logic* 24: 1–14.

Kripke, Saul A. 1963: "Semantical considerations on modal logic", *Acta Philosophica Fennica* 16: 83–94; reprinted 1971 in *Reference and Modality*, ed. Leonard Linsky, Oxford: Oxford University Press, 63–72.

Küng, Guido 1963: *Ontologie und logistische Analyse der Sprache: eine Untersuchung zur zeitgenössischen Universaliendiskussion*, Vienna: Springer.

Lambert, Karel 1958–64: "Notes on 'E!'", *Philosophical Studies* 9: 60–3; 12: 1–5; 13: 51–9; 15: 85–8.

Leibniz, Gottfried Wilhelm von 1686: "Remarks upon Mr Arnaud's letter in regard to my statement that the individual concept of each person involves, once and for all, all that will ever happen to him", in *Basic Writings*, tr. G. R. Montgomery, LaSalle: Open Court, 1902: 103–19.

Leonard, Henry S. 1956: "The logic of existence", *Philosophical Studies* 7: 49–64.

Levinson, Jerrold 1980: "The particularisation of attributes", *Australasian Journal of Philosophy* 58: 102–15.

Lewis, David 1973a: *Counterfactuals*, Cambridge MA: Harvard University Press.

Lewis, David 1973b: "Causation", *Journal of Philosophy* 70: 556–67.

Lewis, David 1979: "Counterpart theory and quantified modal logic", in Loux 1979: 110–28.

Lewis, David 1986: *On the Plurality of Worlds*, Oxford: Blackwell.

Lewis, David 1988: "Parts of classes", departmental seminar, Traditional and Modern Philosophy, University of Sydney, August 1, 1988. (Included in his *Parts of Classes*, Oxford: Blackwell, 1991.)

Locke, John 1689: *An Enquiry concerning Humane Understanding*, London: Thomas Basset, 4 vols.

Lorenzen, Paul 1965: *Differential und Integral: eine konstruktive Einführung in die klassische Analysis*, Frankfurt: Akademische Verlagsgesellschaft; tr. John Bacon, Austin: University of Texas Press, 1972.

Loux, Michael J., ed. 1979: *The Possible and the Actual: Readings in the Metaphysics of Modality*, Ithaca: Cornell University Press.

Lycan, William G. 1979: "The trouble with possible worlds", in Loux 1979: 274–316.

Martin, C. B. 1980: "Substance substantiated", *Australasian Journal of Philosophy* 58: 3–10.

McKinsey, J. C. C. 1949: "A new definition of truth". *Synthese* 7: 428–33.

Menzies, Peter and Price, Huw 1993: "Causation as a secondary quality", *British Journal for the Philosophy of Science* 43.

Moore, G. E. 1912: *Ethics*, Oxford: Clarendon Press.

Ovidius Naso, Publius 1916: *Metamorphoses*, Loeb Classical Library, Cambridge

MA: Harvard University Press.

Palmer, Sally 1989: "Are tropes identical to states of affairs?", essay, fourth-year seminar, Traditional and Modern Philosophy, University of Sydney, November 1989.

Partee, Barbara 1971: "Montague grammar and transformational grammar", Philosophy Department Colloquium, Yale University, New Haven, November 12, 1971. (Published versions omit the discussion of adjectives and adverbs.)

Peirce, C. S. 1931–58: *Collected Papers*, ed. C. Hartshorne and P. Weiss, Cambridge MA: Harvard-Belknap.

Plato 1892: *Timaeus*, in *Works*, tr. Benjamin Jowett, London: Macmillan. Oxford: 1920.

Quine, W. V. 1953a: "On what there is", in *From a Logical Point of View: 9 Logico-Philosophical Essays*, Cambridge MA: Harvard University Press, 1–19.

Quine, W. V. 1953b: "Reference and modality", in *From a Logical Point of View: 9 Logico-Philosophical Essays*, Cambridge MA: Harvard University Press, 139–59.

Quine, W. V. 1960: *Word and Object*, Cambridge MA: MIT.

Ramsey, F. P. 1931: "Universals", in *The Foundations of Mathematics and Other Logical Essays*, ed. R. B. Braithwaite, New York and London: Routledge and Kegan Paul, 270–86. Also in *Philosophical Papers*, ed. D. H. Mellor, Cambridge: Cambridge University Press, 1990: 8–30.

Reid, Thomas 1895: *Essays on the Intellectual Powers of Man*, in *The Works*, vol. I, ed. W. Hamilton, 8th edn, Edinburgh and London: James Thin and Longmans, Green, 219–460.

Routley, Richard 1980: *Exploring Meinong's Jungle and Beyond: An Investigation of Noneism and the Theory of Items*, Philosophy Department, RSSS, Australian National University, Canberra.

Routley, Richard 1989: "Philosophical and linguistic inroads: multiply intensional relevant logics", in *Directions in Relevant Logic*, eds J. Norman and R. Sylvan, Dovdrecht: Kluwer, 269–304.

Routley, R. and Routley, V. 1975: "The role of inconsistent and incomplete theories in the logic of belief", *Communication and Cognition* 8: 185–235.

Russell, Bertrand 1912: "On the notion of cause", in *Mysticism and Logic*, Garden City: Doubleday Anchor, 1957: 174–201.

Russell, Bertrand 1914: *Our Knowledge of the External World*, Chicago: Norton. New York: American Library Mentor Book, 1960.

Russell, Bertrand 1918: "The philosophy of logical atomism", in *Logic and Knowledge: Essays 1901–1950*, ed. R. C. Marsh, London: Allen and Unwin, 1956: 177–281.

Russell, Bertrand 1936: "On order in time", in *Logic and Knowledge: Essays 1901–1950*, ed. R. C. Marsh, London: Allen and Unwin, 1956: 177–281.

Russell, Bertrand 1948: *Human Knowledge: Its Scope and Limits*, London: Allen and Unwin.

Schock, Rolf 1962: "A definition of event and some of its applications", *Theoria* 27: 250–68.

Segerberg, Krister 1973: "Two-dimensional modal logic", *Journal of Philosophical Logic* 2: 77–96.

Sellars, Wilfrid 1962–3: "Classical problems in the theory of knowledge and metaphysics", class, Yale University, New Haven.

Sellars, Wilfrid 1963: "Abstract entities", *Review of Metaphysics* 16: 627–71; reprinted in *Philosophical Perspectives*, Springfield: Charles C Thomas, 1967: 229–69.

Simons, Peter 1995: "Relational tropes", in *Analytic Phenomenology: Essays in Honour of Guido Küng*, ed. G. Haefliger and P. Simons, Dordrecht: Kluwer.

Skyrms, Brian 1989: "Tractarian nominalism", in Armstrong 1989a: 145–52.

Stalnaker, Robert C. 1978: "Assertion", in *Syntax and Semantics 9: Pragmatics*, ed. Peter Cole, New York: Academic Press.

Stelzner, Werner 1992: "Relevant deontic logic", *Journal of Philosophical Logic* 21: 193–216.

Stout, G. F. 1971a: "The nature of universals and propositions", in *The Problems of Universals*, ed. C. Landesman, New York: Basic Books, 154–66.

Stout, G. F. 1971b: "Are the characteristics of particular things universal or particular?", in *The Problems of Universals*, ed. C. Landesman, New York: Basic Books, 178–83.

Thomason, Richmond H. 1969: "Modal logic and metaphysics", in *The Logical Way of Doing Things*, ed. K. Lambert, New Haven: Yale University Press, 119–46.

Thomason, Richmond H. and Stalnaker, Robert C. 1968: "Modality and reference", *Noûs* 2: 359–72.

Trilling, Lionel 1957: *The Middle of the Journey*, Garden City: Doubleday Anchor.

Weinberg, Steven 1977: *The First Three Minutes: A Modern View of the Origin of the Universe*, New York: Basic Books.

Whitehead, Alfred North and Russell, Bertrand 1910–13: *Principia Mathematica*, Cambridge: Cambridge University Press.

Williams, D. C. 1953: "On the elements of being", *Review of Metaphysics* 7: 3–18, 171–92; reprinted as "The elements of being", in *Principles of Empirical Realism*, Springfield: Charles C Thomas, 1966: 74–109. (Later paging cited.)

Williams, D. C. 1986: "Universals and existents", *Australasian Journal of Philosophy* 64: 1–14.

Windelband, Wilhelm 1957: *Lehrbuch der Geschichte der Philosophie*, 15th edn Heinz Heimsoeth, Tübingen: Mohr-Siebeck.

Wittgenstein, Ludwig 1922: *Tractatus Logico-Philosophicus*, tr. C. K. Ogden, London: Trench, Trubner.

Wollheim, Richard 1984: *The Thread of Life*, Cambridge MA: Harvard University Press.

Wright, Georg Henrik von 1951: *An Essay in Modal Logic*, Amsterdam: North-Holland.

Index